WHAT ABOUT IT?

This book comes with my love to ChristaMatts
– the joint youth group of Christ Church and
St Matthew's, Fulham –
who helped me to write it

WHAT ABOUT IT?

LANCE PIERSON

Scripture Union, 207-209 Queensway, Bletchley, Milton Keynes, MK2 2EB, England.

First published 1996
Reprinted 2002

ISBN 1 85999 038 X

Unless otherwise indicated, Scriptures quoted from *The Youth Bible*, New Century Version, copyright © 1991 by Word Publishing, Dallas, Texas 75039. Used by permission.

British Library Cataloguing-in-Publication Data
A catalogue record for this book is available from the British Library.

Cover design by Blue Pig Design Company.
Illustrations by Taffy Davies.

Printed and bound in Great Britain by Cox & Wyman Ltd, Reading, Berkshire.

Scripture Union is an international Christian charity working with churches in more than 130 countries, providing resources to bring the good news about Jesus Christ to children, young people and families and to encourage them to develop spiritually through the Bible and prayer.

As well as our network of volunteers, staff and associates who run holidays, church-based events and school Christian groups, we produce a wide range of publications and support those who use our resources through training programmes.

What's in it

How it all began

This book is a team effort.

Scripture Union wanted a book that answered questions on God and faith that Christians aged 11–14 often ask. So I went to the church youth group I help to lead and asked them what questions they had. We made a list and I had a go at writing some answers. We looked at these together and came up with better answers and a lot more questions!

My friend Nigel Oakley read the first draft, made helpful comments and suggested yet more questions. Scripture Union's editors also sent a batch of further questions.

Back I went to the youth group, and they voted for the order they would like the extra questions squeezed in if there was room. So I would like to give a big thank you to all the members of ChristaMatts who have helped this book come into existence: George Ahad, Kerri Alder, Serena Atkins, Amy Barlow, Rebecca Cummings, Kate Edwards, Zian Embong, Stephen Fowler, Hannah Griffiths, Shanelle Hamilton, Siobhan Luikham, Stephen Matthews, Joy Pierson, Robin Pierson, Carlene Reynolds, Gynette Sharpe, Katherine Soutter, Tom Van Pelt and Susan Yin.

Thank you to John Buckeridge, Editor of *Youthwork*, for his expert advice. And to the members of two Fellowship of Christian Writers' groups (the West of London Regional Group and the Non-fiction Postal Workshop) for their help on the one or two answers I showed them.

Thanks as ever to Yasmin Muttiah, my long-suffering assistant, for doing her usual excellent job looking after the book on computer while it kept changing size and shape.

Thanks above all to Alison Barr, Commissioning Editor at Scripture Union, for her patience during all the to-ing and fro-ing; and for HER wise, encouraging answers to all MY questions about the shape the book should take.

What it's all about

This is a book of questions asked by some friends of mine who are aged between 11 and 14 years old. I've had a shot at answering them. I hope you, and they, find the answers helpful. But if not, all is not lost! By each of the questions there is a **Bible Bit** that gives part of how I think God answers the question. This should be much more helpful than my answer.

But don't just leave it there. It would be good to discuss these questions together with friends, perhaps in a church youth group or school Christian Union if you've got one. At the end of each chapter there are more questions (**Further ???**) for chewing over by yourself or together with others.

And, of course, no answer is ever a FULL answer. It usually just triggers off a set of new questions – which is a good thing. So we've left space for you to record these.

If you get stuck on any questions (ours or yours), why not take them to someone else who could help – perhaps a youth leader, a minister at church or an RE teacher at school? When all else fails, right at the back of the book there is a **Helpline**, showing where you can find further advice with some of the deeper or trickier questions.

Lance Pierson

GOD

Who is God?

There is a very famous bit of the Bible which gives an answer to this question.

David was the greatest king that God's people, Israel, ever had. But before he was king, he was a shepherd boy who looked after sheep in the rough, hilly countryside. So he thought about God in the words and pictures he understood best.

'The LORD is MY shepherd' – David looked after the sheep, but God looked after him. The sheep relied on David to find them food and drink; David relied on God for his. The sheep followed David wherever he led; David looked to God to show him the right way to live. David protected the sheep from their enemies – bears, snakes, poisonous weeds; so he trusted God to keep HIM safe from harm.

God was here before us: he made the universe and everything in it. He is with us now – giving, guiding, guarding. He is out there ahead of us, waiting to welcome us into his house for ever when we reach the end of the road in this life.

I often ask people to write their own version of David's poem, using the words and ideas that mean most to them. I have had several goes myself. At different times I've written 'The Lord is our community police officer', 'The Lord is my team captain', even 'The Lord is my taxi'. But here is the one I would write today. It is based on the most important fact of my life as a child and a young person – I never knew my father. He walked out of my life when I was one.

GOD is my Dad;
   he gives me all I need.
He doesn't shout at me or call me rubbish;
   he says he loves me the way I am.
He fills me with new hope each day,
   and shows me how to make him pleased with all I do in
   it.
Even when I make a mess of things and feel a fool,
   you don't laugh at me, Dad.
You help me get up again
   and bring something good out of my mistakes.
So I don't need to dread tomorrow,
   not even next week or next year.
You're not going to walk out on me;
   You'll stay my Dad for ever.

Why don't you try writing your version of David's psalm?
It will help you understand more clearly what God means
to you.

Psalm 23

The LORD is my shepherd;
   I have everything I need.
He lets me rest in green pastures.
   He leads me to calm water.
He gives me new strength.
He leads me on paths that are right
   for the good of his name.
Even if I walk through a very dark valley,
I will not be afraid,
   because you are with me.
Your rod and your walking stick comfort me.

You prepare a meal for me
   in front of my enemies.
You pour oil on my head;
   you fill my cup to overflowing.

Surely your goodness and love will be with me
    all my life,
and I will live in the house of the LORD forever.

Why does God have to be three people?

It sounds a real puzzler, and it is. God made us and is far, far greater than us – our minds can't take all of him in, certainly not all at once. So he has shown himself to us in three different ways. It is perhaps better to think of it not as three PEOPLE, but as three STAGES.

Sometimes when you try to take a photo of a big view, you can't fit it all into one picture. No problem if you've got a camcorder or a wide-angle lens. But suppose you've only got your little ordinary camera? Don't despair – there's a way round this problem. Take two or more different pictures and then stick them alongside each other in your album. Together they'll make up the full scene. In the same way, God gave us three pictures of himself to make up the complete family portrait.

First, he showed himself in the Old Testament as Father. He chose one man, then his family, then the whole nation that grew from them, and he called this nation his children. He looked after them like a father – feeding and training, protecting and correcting – till they had got that picture of him firmly in their minds.

Then he added a second picture. He came as Jesus and showed himself as the perfect human being. He loved and cared for people day in, day out. He taught his followers how to live the same sort of life as he did. Best of all, he rescued us all from hell by going through it himself on the cross. Then he came back to life to show that he had paid our death penalty in full and we can be forgiven. (To find out more about our sin and why we need God's forgiveness, see pages 13–14.)

My mind is already buzzing! But that is still not the end of God. Now he brings in a third picture. He's not just our

Father in heaven. He is not just Jesus Christ our Lord. From the New Testament onwards he also comes right inside the lives of his people. He wants to be with us the whole time as our friend and leader. So he is also invisible power – God's Spirit in our spirit, the Holy Spirit – making us good and strong to live like Jesus.

Father, Son and Spirit. But not three Gods or three different people. Three names for one and the same God.

Difficult to grasp, but not impossible. God made us, so we have some of his family likeness. In a much smaller way, we are three-but-also-one as well. You are a body and a mind and a spirit, all at the same time. Most activities call all three parts of you into play. Even sitting watching *EastEnders*, you're all there – well, I suppose some people might question that! But what I mean is, your body watches; your mind makes sense of it (or some of it!); your spirit reacts to it (Whose side are you on? Which characters do you like and dislike?).

MY BODY'S WATCHING....
MY MIND'S MAKING SENSE....
.....BUT MY SPIRIT'S STILL
WITH WEST HAM!!

We are high-tech, many-sided creatures. And it takes a many-sided God to meet our needs. When you feel knocked down or upset, our Father God is there to pick you up or calm you down. When you're not sure what to say or do, remember Jesus is with you; he has shown us the perfect way to live, and he wants to help US get it right too. If you feel weak or afraid, the Holy Spirit can top you up with fresh energy and courage. Just ask him.

Bible Bit

Paul hit on the perfect prayer for making sure that we ask for all the help God has got on offer:

The grace of the Lord Jesus Christ, the love of God, and the fellowship of the Holy Spirit be with you all.

If we can never be good enough for God, why should we try?

I once saw a film I won't ever forget. It starred a boy of about 10 or 11, called David. One day, his dad said to him the gross sort of thing some dads do: 'I want to be able to say that I'm proud to be David's dad. Try always to do what will make me proud of you.' Come on, Dad, get real. It's not that easy!

Well, David witnesses a burglary in one of the other flats in the block where they live. The easy thing for him to do would be to creep away and keep quiet about it. But David remembers Dad's words, so he rings the police. Unfortunately, when he goes back to keep watch on the thieves, they catch him and hold him hostage. It all looks pretty hairy for a while, but David manages to keep his cool and, as it's a U film, he gets rescued. Then, what do you know? Dad says he's proud of him.

As Christians we worship OUR Dad too. And he's great, not gross. He made us, and loves us the way he made us.

He loves us so much, he didn't chuck us away when we went wrong. He came as Jesus to take our punishment on himself. Now he offers to forgive us and actually come in on our lives to make a better job of them than we could ourselves. He even says that he wants us to live with him for ever after we die.

Some people can hear all that, and then turn their backs on God and say, 'Get lost. I couldn't care less.'

I can't. OK, I can never be perfect like him. I let him down again and again. It is often a real struggle to do or say what I know I should. But if he loves me enough to die for me and share life with me, I want to learn to love him back, and find out how I can be the kind of person who pleases him.

Who knows? One day he might even be proud of me!

Bible Bit

'Try to please God' was the first lesson that Paul, Silas and Timothy taught the new Christians in one of the first churches they founded:

> We encouraged you, we comforted you, and we kept urging you to live the kind of life that pleases God, who calls you to share in his own Kingdom and glory.

> Brothers and sisters, we taught you how to live in a way that will please God, and you are living that way. Now we ask and encourage you in the Lord Jesus to live that way even more.

How do you know if you have – or haven't – got a relationship with God?

How do you know you've got a relationship with your parent(s) or whoever looks after you at home?

I guess it is a mix of things:

- They have told you that you belong to them.
- They prove it by giving you what you need.
- You spend time together.
- You do some things together.
- You talk to each other, or phone when you're away.
- You love each other, at least some of the time!
- You feel bad when you hurt each other.

You can probably think of other things to add to the list:

Now look at the list again, this time asking, 'How many of these are true of me and God or Jesus?' If none of them is, then perhaps you have never started a relationship with God. It's high time you did! You'll find a prayer you could pray in the **Helpline** on page 127.

If you can see that some or all of the things fit you and God, you've begun to get to know him for yourself. You can be sure he is with you. Prove it by asking him to give you the guts to treat the other people in your life in the way Jesus would – then watch him start to do it.

Bible Bit

If we have got a relationship with God, his Holy Spirit starts to change our character so that it becomes more like God's.

The Spirit produces the fruit of love, joy, peace, patience, kindness, goodness, faithfulness, gentleness and self-control.

What score (out of ten) would you give yourself on each of those qualities?

Further ??? to think about by yourself or discuss with friends

1 When did you begin to think of God as more than just a name? Do you think you have grown to understand him better since then?

2 What would you say to a friend who says, 'Prove to me there's a God'?

3 If God was sitting talking with you now, what questions would you like to ask him? Write them in the space below.

4 God sometimes begins to answer our questions in our minds even while we are still writing them down. If this has happened with you, what do you see as his answer to (some of) the questions you wrote in **3** above?

PRAYER

Does God always hear you when you pray?

We had a teacher at school who used to test our knowledge out loud with questions like 'What is the capital of Portugal?' or 'What is the square root of 81?' If we shouted out 'Lisbon!' or 'Nine!', he always looked at the wall and said, 'I can't hear you.'

Of course, he could really – there was nothing wrong with his hearing – but he was teaching us the rules. He wanted us to stick up a hand and wait for him to say whose turn it was to answer.

Prayer is sometimes a bit like that. God CAN hear every prayer ever prayed. He has got the best hearing in the universe. We don't have to say the words out loud: he can 'hear' our thoughts. We don't even have to use words at all: he can 'hear' our feelings.

But sometimes he says he DOESN'T hear our prayers or, rather, they 'turn him off' and he won't say 'Yes' to them. If our prayers are selfish, for instance: 'God, make me top scorer in the match, the most popular person in the class, and – while you're at it – a millionaire'. Or if our prayers are full of hate instead of love: 'Lord, give her a taste of her own medicine. Look what she said about me. I'll never forgive her. I'll get my own back'. God understands how we feel; he wants to comfort us and help us get over our hurts. But he won't have anything to do with that sort of prayer.

Jesus taught us the Lord's Prayer to show the kind of prayer God wants to hear. This doesn't mean you can only pray the exact words of the Lord's Prayer. You're welcome to use your own words and ideas any time you like, but Jesus' prayer sets the pattern. Make your prayers like his.

'Hallowed be your name, your kingdom come, your will be done'

Please God, make everything turn out the way you want. Only give me what I want if it's what YOU want for me. Do what makes you pleased, because that is what's best for me. The same goes for everyone else you want me to pray for.

'Give us today our daily bread'

Remind me that everything we need really comes from you: not just food, but health, family, friends, money, fun, knowledge, skills, making good choices in all the things I have to make up my own mind about. Please God, give me what I NEED, especially when it's not the same as what I WANT.

'Forgive us our sins ... as we forgive others'

Here is a prayer God will always hear. It is really important to get right with him when we've done or said or thought something wrong. Sometimes just the one word – 'Sorry' – is enough. But here Jesus expects our 'Sorry' prayers to be in two parts:

1 'Sorry I swore at him/her…'
2 'I give up being angry at him/her for joking about me.'

We can't ask God to forgive us if we won't forgive other people. It is hard, but God will help us. Go on, try it.

'Deliver us from evil'

Once you have said you're truly sorry and are willing to forgive, God has heard; he has forgiven you – get up and go on. But ask him to help you not to make the same mistake again. On our own we are weak, and the devil always wants to trip us up. So ask God to keep you on the right tracks with him.

These are prayers God will always hear: he LOVES to hear them. 'It's good to talk' on the phone, but it's even better to talk with God. He is our Dad. He wants us to get to know him better; to share all our feelings with him – happy and sad, hopes and fears.

What a great God! Why not add one other prayer he'll always hear – 'THANKS!'

Bible Bit

Isaiah says there are times when God doesn't hear us:

> Don't think that the LORD is too weak to save you or too deaf to hear your call for help! It is because of your sins that he doesn't hear you. It is your sins that separate you from God when you try to worship him.

But David says we can be sure God will hear us if…

> The LORD is close to everyone who prays to him,
> to all who truly pray to him.
> He gives those who respect him what they want.
> He listens when they cry, and he saves them.

Does God give us everything we pray for?

Not if it would be bad for us, like a win on the lottery which is too big to handle. Not if it's something that goes against the way God has made the world, like brilliant exam results without doing any work, or your team automatically winning every match it plays.

Not if it means stamping out other people's freedom of action. This is why we don't see the whole world at peace even though we pray for it again and again. Sadly, there are people who choose to fight because they think it is the only way to get what they want. God doesn't magically stop them because then they would be zombies and not people.

So what DOES God give us when we pray?

He gives us what he has promised to give us: things like forgiveness, help when we need it, wisdom to know the right thing to do and the strength to do it (see 1 John 1:9; Hebrews 4:16; James 1:5; 1 Corinthians 10:13). All the other things we pray for – good weather, good health or recovery for those who are ill, safety when travelling, friends we would like to become Christians – we have to wait to see how God will answer. He certainly does answer, but he won't always say 'Yes'. Sometimes he says 'No' or at least 'Not yet'. Sometimes he says 'Yes, but in a different way'.

He doesn't always give us what we want. He gives us what HE wants, and surely that's the best answer possible.

Bible Bit

The only way to be sure of getting what we pray for is to pray for what God wants:

> And this is the boldness we have in God's presence: that if we ask God for anything that agrees with what he wants, he hears us. If we know he hears us every time we ask him, we know we have what we ask from him.

Jesus tells us the only way to be sure of asking for what God wants:

> 'If you remain in me and follow my teachings, you can ask anything you want, and it will be given to you.'

What if someone you know dies even if you've prayed for them? How could God allow this to happen?

This is just the sort of prayer where we have to wait to see whether God answers 'Yes', 'No' or 'Yes but in a different way'.

Obviously, we long for him to say 'Yes'. When I was at college, I belonged to the student Christian Union. One member had a younger brother, still at school, who got cancer. We prayed and prayed, and so did many others, but Graham got steadily worse and finally died – aged 17.

It felt desperate for us as helpless onlookers. Graham was a Christian and his faith held up, but there must have been moments when he felt angry and cheated of the long life everyone expects. His family and friends were totally gutted at losing him so soon. We felt God had said 'No' to our prayers. He could have healed Graham. So why didn't he?

This is probably the toughest question in this book, and I don't know the whole answer. God's mind is much too big for us to know everything in it. I think part of the answer is that God can see the other side of death, while we can't.

For God, death isn't a solid brick wall: it's a gateway through to the garden on the other side of the wall. It isn't like the end of a film: it's like the end of this week's episode in a soap or serial – TO BE CONTINUED...

This life isn't the only one. God is planning a new world where there will be no more dying and crying. If someone leaves this life early – especially if they are a Christian – it isn't the end of their story. With God in their life, it just means they are moving from the caterpillar stage to become a butterfly forever (see 1 Corinthians 15:51–55). By dying and going to heaven, Graham HAD got better – better even than we had prayed for.

The other day I met a lady whose job is to care for people who have just had a death in the family. She was visiting a widow who was in such a state of shock that it was as if she had just come out of the freezer: 'My husband was only in his 40s. Why has God let him die so young?'

'What work did he do?' the carer asked her.

'He was a gardener for the council.'

The picture of a garden gave the carer an idea of what to say next: 'Did he have a garden of his own?'

'Yes, out the back.'

'Did he ever pick flowers for you?'

'Yes, the first ones that came out. He always said they were best.'

'Do you think perhaps God saw your husband as a fine new flower? Perhaps he is now part of a great new flower arrangement in heaven.'

God hadn't said 'No' to this woman's prayer. He had said 'Yes – but in a different, even better way'. She had prayed for her husband to get better. God did more than that: he made her husband fitter and stronger than he had ever been before. In heaven he will never be ill or weak or in pain again.

But this may sound like a mean trick. She wanted her husband back with her – alive not dead. I said it was a tough question!

We have got to remember the things we have seen already. GOD rules the world, not us. If we could get everything we prayed for, it would be US in charge. God doesn't always give us what we want: he gives us what HE wants. Sometimes what he wants is very painful. However, even if we can't see how, it is for our good. A filling at the dentist's is painful, but it's better than losing the tooth. God could see the woman's husband was ready for heaven, and (I guess) that she would only grow into a better, more complete person without him. But, of course, she will only come to understand this later.

God can't really be accused of being mean and unfeeling. He feels the pain as much as we do, probably more. All the things that cause early death – cancer, AIDS, smoking, drug and alcohol abuse, pollution, bad diet, bad driving, wars and terrorist bombs – they hurt God and he hates them.

Of course, he COULD abolish these things just like that, and I am far from understanding fully why he doesn't (see Jeremiah 32:17). But I think there may be one reason. Have you ever thought what would happen if God did stop or reverse tragedies for Christians when they prayed? I think it would actually cause Christianity to die out.

For one thing, if people discovered that God made Christians automatically safe from cancer, they would all become 'Christians' overnight. If the only reason for their conversion was to have guaranteed good health, what sort of Christians would they be? Would they love Jesus? Or want to obey his commands? How would 'real' Christians learn to be better Christians if they were surrounded by 'pretend' ones? Wouldn't they just stop being real Christians themselves?

If, for example, God used miracles to protect all Christians from car accidents, we would become complete road-hogs. If we knew we could never hurt anyone, however hard we attacked them, we would never grow out of the rages and fits we had as toddlers. We would be totally selfish. We would never learn to care about other people. Christianity would disappear, and so would everything else good in life. Good qualities like love, peace, patience, kindness, gentleness and self-control simply wouldn't exist.

However, if God tried to get round this by programming us to stay nice and Christian, we would be robots not human beings. God doesn't want mindless machines in his family; he wants us to be his children who learn to love him in response to his great love for us.

So rather than 'magic' the nasty side of life away, God sees that it is often better for us to go through it. But he doesn't leave us to go it alone. He promises to come with us through the horrors. He shares the pain with us. He builds up our strength to cope. He uses our experience to teach us to care for others. In particular, he wants us to care for the people left behind when their loved ones die, like the widow my friend cared for (see James 1:27).

Bible Bit

Jesus promised that his followers would have life after death because he conquered death himself:

> 'I am the resurrection and the life. Those who believe in me will have life even if they die.'

All Christians can rely on God's promise to be with us at all times:

> God has said,
> 'I will never leave you;
> I will never forget you.'
> So we can be sure when we say:
> 'I will not be afraid, because the Lord is my helper.
> People can't do anything to me.'

James even tells us to be glad when we suffer, because we can be sure God will make us better Christians through it:

> My brothers and sisters, when you have many kinds of troubles, you should be full of joy, because you know that these troubles test your faith, and this will give you patience. Let your patience show itself perfectly in what you do. Then you will be perfect and complete and will have everything you need.

How is it possible for God to hear all our prayers at once?

When I was a child, I used to think God had a huge switchboard with a little light for every person in the world. When we prayed, on would go our light on his board. He would then flick on his earphones and listen in.

I still think this isn't a bad picture. God is always there, ready to hear and talk and help. He never gives us the busy engaged tone like when you try to get through to a really popular phone-in. God is what they call 'INFINITE' – he can do any number of things at the same time. He has got enough lines to hear everyone who calls on him at the same moment. Enough vision to see us all at once. Enough brainpower to work out every problem and need. Enough energy to send a message or deliver the resources straightaway.

God knows everything, sees everything, hears everything, can do everything – except go against his own loving nature. So keep praying!

Bible Bit

The psalm-writer Asaph encourages us from his experience of God:

> I cry out to God;
> I call to God, and he will hear me.

The angel Gabriel sums up the vast mysteries of God in just four words:

> God can do anything!

I'm too busy to stop and pray. Is it OK to pray while I do my homework?

It's GREAT to pray while you're doing your homework, as

long as you're praying about the homework. God is interested in what you do (even when you aren't!) and wants to help you do it well.

I don't think it is such a good idea to leave all your other prayers – about your family and friends and people in need – until homework time. It sounds like a recipe for putting homework off, or for doing both things (homework and prayer) badly.

God wants to hear from you often, about anything that matters to you: worries and upsets certainly, but also the good things like friends, family, school, TV, music, interests, things in the news. He is ready for you to contact him any time, anywhere, whenever you feel the need.

However, if this sort of 'instant prayer' is to work, we also need to have a regular prayer time every so often. My electric razor is ready to use every day, but only because I give it a recharge once a week. We all need 'recharge prayer' when we have time to listen to God as well as talk to him. This could be once or twice a week, perhaps at a church service. Or it could be every day, reading a bit of the Bible, with help from Scripture Union notes like *One Up* (see **Helpline** on page 127 for further info). Or it could be a few minutes' quiet BEFORE YOU START your homework.

But don't say you're too busy. Are you too busy to eat? Or go out with friends? Or have a birthday party? Prayer is meeting GOD who made the world and looks after it! Too busy to meet HIM?!

Bible Bit

Jesus encouraged us to ask God for everything we need, but also to have a definite time and place to pray:

> 'When you pray, you should go into your room and close the door and pray to your Father who cannot be seen. Your Father can see what is done in secret, and he will reward you.'

If you need help, and God knows what has happened because he can read your mind, does he still help you even though you haven't prayed for help?

Not automatically.

God knows the help we need even before we do, and he often gives it to us without us getting round to asking.

This must happen more often than we realise. The other day, my bike-chain snapped as I was cycling round Hyde Park Corner, probably the busiest roundabout in London. This might have been really nasty, as the traffic usually sweeps down on you three lanes deep. 'Help!' I squeaked. But God was already there. That precise moment was unusually quiet with just one car in sight. The driver was able to stop and let me run for safety to the pavement.

But sometimes God doesn't step in first. He waits for us to ask. This is partly to teach us and remind us that we need to trust him. We can't rely on 'good luck' or our own cleverness. Partly too because he wants to hear from us. Prayer is one way we get to know God better and love him more. What sort of friendship do you have with people you never speak to?

Bible Bit

God told Isaiah how thoroughly he would look after his people:

> 'I will provide for their needs before they ask,
>   and I will help them while they are still asking for
>   help.'

However, James told his Christian readers that God sometimes waits to be asked:

> You do not get what you want, because you do not ask
> God.

How do you know what job to do?

As Christians, we have obeyed Jesus' call to follow him. This means he has taken charge of every part of our lives. He has a really good life mapped out for each of us to live, and this includes the work or job we will do after we leave school or college.

I say work OR job, because there aren't enough paid jobs to go round and some people have to do without. This doesn't mean they DON'T work. People who stay at home and look after their house or children or sick relatives often work much harder than those of us with jobs. Others do unpaid work for hospitals or charities or churches which is incredibly valuable; the whole place would fold without them.

As Christians, we are learning to fit into God's plans, and this might mean unpaid work rather than a paid job. Keep your mind open to all the possibilities.

So, how do we find out what sort of work – paid or unpaid – God wants us to do? The first thing is to keep the right attitude. That means praying about it. Ask God to lead you along his path. Put the whole process into his hands. Trust him to have it all under control.

Then – WITH THAT ATTITUDE – use the normal system which is there to help you. Most schools have teachers giving advice on careers. They will ask first if there is anything you WANT to do. If there is, it's worth looking at – if you like the idea, you may well be good at it. (Sadly, of course, you may not be. I wanted to play cricket for England, but it didn't take long to realise it wasn't on. I wasn't even good enough to play for the school.)

The careers advisor will then look at what you ARE good at, what you are interested in, and what you enjoy. This will help them suggest the kind of work that fits your sort of person. They will have the information to tell you how to find out more about anything you think is worth exploring.

Another approach is to visit a local jobcentre, where they

list what jobs are going in the area. And there are lots of job adverts in newspapers. This is how I found my first job. As I couldn't get the really top job (professional cricketer), I decided to aim lower and be a teacher! I felt I had some clue what to do because I had just spent seventeen years in schools and college watching teachers trying to do it!

I am still a teacher of sorts. Not in a school, but in churches and adult education colleges, teaching through books and drama and training courses. Each time I have changed direction or taken on a new job, I have felt excited: 'This is what I really want to do'. I don't think this is being selfish. I think it's the way God shows us that we are doing the work he made us for.

Bible Bit

Paul reminds us God is in control:

> God has made us what we are. In Christ Jesus, God made us to do good works, which God planned in advance for us to live our lives doing.

According to David, if our attitude to God is right, our ambitions will fit in with his plans:

> Seek your happiness in the LORD,
>   and he will give you your heart's desire.
> Give yourself to the LORD;
>   trust in him, and he will help you...

David also gives us a model prayer to pray:

> LORD ...
>   show me the right thing to do.
> Show me clearly how you want me to live.

Further ??? to think about by yourself or discuss with friends

1 What do you find a helpful way to pray? Are there specially good times and places?

2 Have there been times when you were sure God heard and answered your prayer? And times when it seems he didn't? How did these times make you feel?

3 If God was sitting talking with you now, what questions about prayer would you like to ask him? Write them in the space below.

Could you turn some of these questions into a prayer now?

4 What other prayers would you say to God if you could see him and hear him?
  Why not pray some of them now, even though you can't see or hear him?

THE BIBLE

Who created the Bible and wrote it?

About forty different people WROTE the Bible, but I think it was God who CREATED it. Without always realising it, the Bible writers were working to his plan.

In one sense, the Bible isn't just one book: it is a collection of sixty-six books inside the same cover. The very word 'Bible' means 'BOOKS', not 'book'. The Bible needs to be many books because it is a long-running story spanning two thousand years. It is like a TV soap, telling the story of one family – in fact, you could call it 'The Family'. After a few background episodes about the beginning of the world, it homes in on one man, Abraham, then follows the story of his children and descendants till they have a whole country of their own.

The Family has an invisible and invincible secret: although Abraham seems like the founding father, the real Father of the family is God. He stays alive and in charge through every generation. Near the end of the story he introduces a dramatic twist in the plot. In the old days, only Abraham's birth descendants could be part of the family. Then one day, God starts adopting children from all countries under the sun.

This, of course, is where we come in. Once the Bible has got this bigger, speedily growing family off the ground, it fades out and leaves up-to-date episodes of 'The Family' to us, and to our Father-God.

The Bible is like our own family history. You could, of course, have one writer telling it all in about AD 100, but it's more real and up-to-the-minute the way God did it. He had reporters at each of the key stages. So we have Moses and David and Paul and Luke and the rest all writing their part of the story around the time it happened.

Although these reporters wrote different episodes and songs and letters, you could say that the Bible is one book after all. It has one main story-line: God builds up his family and looks after it through a never-ending series of adventures and dangers. There is one main character: God himself – Father, Son and Holy Spirit. There has never been another book like it – put together by forty different writers on the job for 1,500 years. It is the greatest book in the world, the all-time best seller. No writer today even DREAMS of staying in print for two thousand years and being translated into every language under the sun. I can only think of one way to explain the Bible's amazing success. Behind all the human scriptwriters, God was at work as the Editor and Director-in-Chief. He made sure they said what he wanted, to bring the whole thing together into one mega epic. This is why Christians believe the Bible is not just another book; it is God's Book.

Bible Bit

Peter explains this fact of God controlling the parts of the Bible called prophecy; but it is also true of the whole thing:

> For no prophetic message (in the scriptures) ever came just from human will, but people were under the control of the Holy Spirit as they spoke the message that came from God.

Why are there so many versions?

For centuries the English-speaking world made do with the 'Authorised Version' of the Bible. It is sometimes called the

'King James Version' after James I who had it translated into English in 1611. So it is nearly 400 years old now and sounds very olde Englishe indeed. No wonder there has been a flood of new translations in this century, to help us read the Bible in modern language. But why so many different modern versions? A friend of mine at college had eleven different translations of the Bible on her bookshelf!

I think one reason is the way the English language keeps changing so fast. Every year there are new 'in' words and old words slightly change their meaning. For a long time, the English word 'man' translated two different words in the Hebrew and Greek languages in which the Bible was first written. One word for 'man' meant a male human being; the other meant the whole human race or mankind. The *Good News* Bible first came out in 1976. At that time it could translate the Hebrew of Psalm 8 like this:

> **When I look at the sky, which you have made,**
> **at the moon and the stars, which you set in their**
> **places –**
> **what is man, that you think of him;**
> **mere man, that you care for him?**

We can't use 'man' like this any more, because it appears to leave girls and women out. So, by 1994, a second edition was needed, which translates as:

> **what are human beings, that you think of them;**
> **mere mortals, that you care for them?**

However, this translation still follows closely the way that Hebrew poetry thinks and speaks. Even the *Good News* Bible isn't always easy for young people to read. Many people felt we needed a still clearer, simpler translation. So, in 1993, *The Youth Bible* was produced, using the New Century Version, which tries to put 'God's Word in understandable language throughout the world'.

Here is how this version translates the same two verses:

> **I look at your heavens,**
> **which you made with your fingers.**
> **I see the moon and stars,**
> **which you created.**
> **But why are people important to you?**
> **Why do you take care of human beings?**

Compare it with the *Good News* Bible. Which do you find easier to follow? Which do you prefer? Do you think it's good to have both versions around to choose between?

Is the Bible all true?

The copy of the Bible I am using for this book has got 1,347 pages in it. But when people ask 'Is it all true?', they aren't usually worried about 1,200 pages of it.

They're only thinking about the first 5 pages (God making the world and the human race), perhaps the last 14 pages (John's glimpse into the future), and about 130 pages in the middle which record Jesus' miracles. Let's look at them one by one.

In the beginning

Many people wonder if the Bible has got it right when it tells us that God made the world in seven days and started the human race with Adam and Eve (see Genesis 1 and 3).

The trouble is, even your great-granddad wasn't alive then so no one knows anything for sure, not even the scientists. Good scientists are quite ready to admit they haven't PROVED how the world began. They can only put together their best guess from the information we've got so far.

It is all so long ago, we're not even sure what sort of information the Bible is giving us. It may be a detailed historical record of exactly what happened. Or it may be a simplified summary.

When a very small child asks, 'Where did I come from?', we usually say, 'Out of Mummy's tummy.' We may even explain that they grew out of the seed Daddy planted in Mummy's tummy. But we probably don't go into the full details of love and sex! That will come later. What we tell them is perfectly true; it's just not the whole story. We tell them as much as they can take in for now.

In the same way, God may have given us an easy-to-understand version of where the human race came from. If he gave us the full technical details, even university professors wouldn't understand it. But we can all see what he is getting at when he says he made the universe in steady, well-planned stages, where each 'day' may be a 24-hour unit or may stand for a much longer period or age. (There is more about this in the question 'Is it OK to believe in evolution as a Christian?' on page 50.)

Deep down we know what he means when he says the first human beings went wrong by doing the one thing he told them not to do, with the result that he shut them out of his Garden. We know this is true because we know we do the same. Until Jesus comes and puts things right between us and God, we feel just as cut off from God as Adam and Eve did.

In the end

The other end of the Bible is also a bit blurred and out of focus. In the book called Revelation, God reveals to John what is going on in the universe beyond our world of time and space. It isn't always easy to know which bits are past, present or future. Because Revelation is a vision (rather like a dream), a lot of the characters appear in code or picture-language. For example, Jesus appears sometimes as a burning man like the Human Torch, sometimes as a Lamb (see Revelation 1:12–16; 5:6–10).

But the overall picture is clear. A spiritual battle has been raging since human beings rebelled against God. The devil wants to take us all with him to hell. But Jesus defeated him on the cross by taking the penalty we deserve for all the wrong things we have done. Now Jesus and his forces are wiping up the opposition as they advance towards the new heaven and earth. These events will fall into place when Jesus comes back to the world. We don't know when that will be: it could be any moment, so we had better be ready!

Some people say this is a load of rubbish, but I'm quite sure it's true. The old part of the Bible gave a stack of predictions about Jesus coming to earth the first time. (See Matthew 1:22–23; 2:5–6, 15; 3:17; 27:35, 39, 43, 46 just for starters. Matthew was especially keen to show how the old predictions of Jesus came true.) They all turned out 100 per cent accurate. Why should it – and Jesus himself – be wrong when they predict that he will come a second time?

Miracles

There are three other parts of the Bible (as well as the life of Jesus) where God is shown working miracles – in the lives of Moses (crossing the Red Sea), Elijah and Elisha (Elijah being fed by ravens), and the apostles (Paul healing people). But the Gospels show Jesus performing more miracles than any of the others.

Here again we can't know for sure (in this life) whether

these miracles happened, because we weren't there. But if Jesus is who he said he is – God's Son, no less – what's so strange about him being able to control the 'laws' of nature? He invented them, after all. In any case, they aren't the sort of laws no one can ever break. They are simply how things usually happen. In normal conditions, for example, people can't walk on water or bring dead bodies back to life. But Jesus is God as well as a human being. He can call on God's super-powers. If you or I could walk across Lake Galilee or command Lazarus to come out of his grave, it certainly would be a miracle. But with Jesus, doing things like that comes naturally because of who he is. I would find it a lot harder to believe if he DIDN'T perform any miracles.

And aren't Jesus' miracles just the sort of thing you would expect God to do? They helped and healed people. Jesus didn't strike people blind; he made them see. He didn't let them starve; he fed them. That's the sort of God who I know deep down must be real. It all rings true to me.

Bible Bit

Psalm 119 is a love song to God for the Bible (the part of it that had been written by then):

> **Your goodness continues for ever,**
> **and your teachings are true.**

Jesus echoed the psalm the night before he died in his prayer to God for all his followers:

> **'Make them ready for your service through your truth;**
> **your teaching is truth.'**

How do we know the writers didn't change the facts or exaggerate them?

Once again, we won't know FOR CERTAIN till we can ask

God in heaven. But there is very strong evidence that the Bible facts are true. They were written down while the people who saw what happened were still alive. Lots of people heard Jesus speak and saw what he did. IF THE WRITERS OF THE GOSPELS HAD ALTERED OR EXAGGERATED EVENTS, THESE WITNESSES WOULD HAVE SAID SO.

The Gospels were written about thirty years after Jesus' death, which may seem a long time for people to remember the events. But they were writing down what they had been preaching every day since Pentecost – which was only seven weeks after Easter.

In the same way, Paul records the main events about Jesus in one of his letters:

> **Christ died for our sins ... he was buried and was raised to life on the third day ... he was seen by Peter and then by the twelve apostles. After that, Jesus was seen by more than five hundred of the believers at the same time. Most of them are still living today...**

Paul wrote this about twenty-three years after Jesus died, but he says that those are the facts he told the people he was writing to WHEN HE FIRST VISITED THEM ('I want you to remember the Good News I brought to you'). That was six years before he wrote, and only seventeen years after Jesus died.

More than that, he says they are the same facts HE WAS TOLD when he became a Christian sixteen years earlier still ('I passed on to you what I received'). This was within two years of Jesus dying, and takes us back so close to the event itself that it would be impossible to change anything.

How can God speak to me through the Bible?

You may have heard people talk about God 'speaking' to them through the Bible. This can be quite a puzzling idea the first time you think about it.

It doesn't mean that God speaks the words out loud as we look at them. And definitely not that we should let the Bible's pages fall open anywhere and then take the first words our eyes see as God's message to us.

Somebody once tried this, but was a bit alarmed when he read, 'Judas went off and hanged himself'. He thought he had better try again, but this time the book fell open at 'Then go and do what he did'. He hardly dared to look again, but felt that he couldn't leave things where they were. So he tried once more: 'The thing that you will do – do it quickly' (see Matthew 27:5; Luke 10:37; John 13:27). He decided – quite rightly – that this isn't the way God speaks to us!

We get closer to the answer when we work out why God had the Bible put together. Paul made it very clear when he said, 'All Scripture [another name for the Bible] is given by God and is useful' – then he listed the four things God wants to do to us through the Bible (see 2 Timothy 3:16):

1 teach the truth;
2 show people what is wrong in their lives;
3 correct faults;
4 teach how to live right.

How does this work? The Bible reading and talk at my church yesterday contained these words of Paul:

> **So you must stop telling lies. Tell each other the truth, because we all belong to each other in the same body.**

This clearly SHOWS SOMETHING WRONG – telling lies. It shows how to CORRECT IT – stop! It TEACHES HOW TO LIVE RIGHT – tell the truth. It also teaches why God wants us to live that way – we all belong in the same body. Christians belong to each other like your hand belongs to your arm. Just think how your body would collapse if its communication system started feeding in lies. What would happen to you if your eyes told your feet, 'No, this isn't a lorry approaching at speed. It's quite OK for you to cross the road now'? Or if your stomach said to your mouth, 'I know I haven't had anything to eat all day, but I don't feel at all hungry'? The body depends totally on truth.

Yesterday God was telling me that the church needs truth just as much. Already today I've been tempted to tell a lie to someone who belongs to our church. I nearly gave in to the temptation, but God reminded me what he said yesterday and I've asked him to forgive me and give me strength to live right.

God actually speaking to ME through the words in the Bible which he masterminded! This is really exciting. Exciting but a bit uncomfortable at times, because it includes showing up my faults and correcting them.

Of course, it is not always so obvious what the Bible means. So I recommend three helpful tips.

1 Get help to know which bit of the Bible to read.

If you're in a church or group study, someone else has usually chosen the Bible passage already. But if you're reading on your own, the best way I know is to use Scripture Union's *One Up* booklets. (Look up the **Helpline** on page 127 to find out where to get them.) They give you a bit of the Bible for each day, then a short note to help you work out what it means.

2 Use an easy-to-read version of the Bible.

I recommend either of the versions we have used for this book: *The Youth Bible* and the *Good News* Bible.

3 Pray before you start.

(Do this whether you're reading the verses yourself or listening to someone else explain them.) Ask God to help you understand this part of his Book. He had it put there in the first place; now he wants to say something to you through it. He is with you as you read or listen.

Can God speak to me through dreams?

He certainly can. He spoke to several people in the Bible through dreams. He used dreams four times to protect the baby Jesus (see Matthew 1:20; 2:12,13,19,22). And Joseph and Daniel had the ability to explain what God was saying through other people's dreams.

But, throughout the Bible and even today, God seems only to speak through dreams to a few special people. You may be one of them. If so, I'm sure it would be good to make a note of your dreams and ask an older Christian if they agree with what you think God is saying through them.

There may be other ways God is sharing his thoughts and ideas with you. It may not be dreams in your sleep, but a vision while you are awake. This can be a word or picture or deep ambition which won't leave you alone. Here again, see if another Christian can help you understand what God wants you to do next.

However, I don't think any of these has ever been God's usual way of speaking to most of his people for most of the time. Most of us have forgotten the dreams we have each night by the time we wake up. Even the few we do remember are often a case of what the Bible calls 'bad dreams come from too much worrying' (see Ecclesiastes 5:3). Our minds churn on while we're asleep and can come up with pretty weird fantasies.

The way God speaks to most Christians most of the time is through the Bible. That is where he has had everything he wants us to learn put on record.

Further ??? to think about by yourself or discuss with friends

1 What is one of your favourite Bible bits? Look it up if you know where to find it. What do you think God wants you to learn from it?

2 Are there any bits of the Bible you find hard to understand or believe? Who might be able to help you with them?

3 How could you try to answer a friend who says, 'The Bible's a load of rubbish'?

4 If you have thought of any more questions after reading this section, make a note of them here. Then why not discuss them with another Christian, a youth leader or your church minister?

CHRISTIANITY AND OTHER RELIGIONS

Does the Bible say you have to go to church?

No. Some people can't get to church meetings. They're in hospital, or they've got jobs where they have to work on Sundays. You yourself may belong to a school or sports club which wants you to train or go out on trips at the same time that your church youth group meets.

But what if you haven't got a really strong reason for missing church?

The Bible does expect EVERY CHRISTIAN WHO CAN to be there when church members get together. Jesus went every week to the synagogue (this is what Jewish people call their church meeting, see Luke 4:16). This isn't because God wants to bore us stiff or stop us having fun. It is because we need it. Christians need church as much as we all need food to eat or air to breathe.

Have you noticed how your faith is stronger after a good Sunday service or youth group meeting? God seems closer, you love him more, you want to pray to him. But, if you drift away from other Christians, you drift away from God as well. You think about him less and less, and you stop living like a Christian.

This is because God has made every Christian part of a team, to play together and help each other become better Christians. If you are a Christian, you need the others and they need you. Just by being there, you make everyone else that little bit more sure that God is alive and true. By taking part in all that goes on, you learn more about Jesus yourself, and you help the others to learn.

What would happen if two or three key players in a sports team you support didn't bother to turn up? The Bible doesn't say the England football team have got to go to Wembley, but I guess you would have a job stopping them. And the team manager might have a thing or two to say if they didn't.

In the same way, OUR Team Manager wants US there when the church family get together to cheer for him and learn from him. He has selected us to play against the devil's opposition.

God may even want you to pull out of any other Sunday clubs you belong to (at least for a time). Try asking him about it. And perhaps ask one or two other church members for their advice. This is what you need them for.

Bible Bit

Let us think about each other and help each other to show love and do good deeds. You should not stay away from the church meetings, as some are doing, but you should meet together and encourage each other.

44

What if your church is really boring?

I'm glad to say that many churches try to include the needs and ideas of their young people when they make their plans and decisions. But there are still some which seem boring to people in their teens. This is partly because adults are often in charge, and they tend to do things more slowly.

Partly too because churches (and other religions) are trying to do something really unusual. I don't know any other club or group which tries to get together people of every age from the youngest baby to the oldest granny. It's like a massive family party where you have got to find something enjoyable for everyone to do.

The answer is to spend some of the time in smaller groups with people the same age as you. Many churches manage to run a teenage youth fellowship. If yours doesn't, perhaps you could start one with some friends, or with another church nearby. Or what about a Christian group at school? (If you would like help with this, see the **Helpline** on page 127.) Small groups should be able to give you the support and sharing, and some of the learning you need to keep growing as a Christian. This is what Jesus wants 'church' to mean for you. When the Bible talks about church, it doesn't mean a MEETING we have to go to. It means a FAMILY OF PEOPLE we belong to – automatically, because they are all Jesus' sisters and brothers just as we are. We would be a strange family if we didn't get to know each other and love each other. We can only do this if we meet at least once a week or so.

Bible Bit

Jesus looks on us, his followers, as an even closer family than his birth mother and brothers were:

> 'My true brother and sister and mother are those who do what God wants.'

Why are there so few Christians at school?

There may be more than you think. Some people are real Christians who love Jesus, who join in with other Christians at home and church – but they never let on at school. They keep quiet in RE about what they really believe, and they don't go to the school Christian Union. They're afraid they will be laughed at or pushed around.

And, of course, they might be. It is a risk that Jesus expects all Christians to take. He asks us to have the courage to be his disciples all day EVERY day. This means being fair and kind to everyone we come across – even the ones who are unpopular at school. It means telling the truth – even saying, 'Yes, I'm a Christian', if someone asks you.

It's tough. Jesus never pretended it would be easy to follow him, which is why only a small percentage of people in Britain have got the guts to be true Christians. It is probably less than 10 per cent and probably about the same in school – perhaps two or three people in each class on average.

Jesus wants it to be more, and in many parts of the world – like Africa and South America and South Korea – it is FAR more. So why not here too? Let's stop limping along at the back.

Growth starts with you and me. If we follow Jesus faithfully, it will challenge others to start following too.

What if you grow up to believe in another god, and then convert to Christianity but still believe in the other god?

You will probably always value the good and helpful things about the way you were brought up. I know of a Jewish lady who became a Christian and married a Christian minister. But she still gives her children a special 'sabbath' family time and meal on Friday nights, because she loved that part of her own Jewish childhood.

Bible Bit

Jesus told his followers to recruit others:

> 'All power in heaven and on earth is given to me. So go and make followers of all people in the world.'

He called following him 'true life', but he admitted that it was tough:

> 'If people want to follow me, they must give up the things they want. They must be willing even to give up their lives to follow me. Those who want to save their lives will give up true life. But those who give up their lives for me and for the Good News will have true life.'

Jesus realised he would never appeal to the majority:

> 'Enter through the narrow gate. The gate is wide and the road is wide that leads to hell, and many people enter through that gate. But the gate is small and the road is narrow that leads to true life. Only a few people find that road.'

In the same way, I hope that a converted Buddhist would go on caring for the natural world around them; and a converted Muslim would go on taking a strong stand against drunkenness or sex outside marriage. These are good things in their old religions.

But, if they have become Christians, they can't go on worshipping the old god in the same way. They will now want to worship Jesus. He is God's only Son – the only person who was God and a human being at the same time.

Jews and Muslims believe in the Old Testament, so when they become Christians they may well think of Jesus as improving or completing their old faith. He shows them clearly the God they always believed in. But Hindus believe in many different gods, and Buddhists in no god at all. So

when they become Christians they start thinking in a totally new way. Like all of us, they learn to see Jesus in charge
of every part of their lives.

Most of us had beliefs of our own before we started following Jesus. They seemed like a torch or night-light helping us to see a little in the dark. But meeting Jesus is like
drawing back the curtains to find that it is morning. Who
needs the lights on in the brilliant midday sun?

Bible Bit

Jesus made huge claims about himself. If he's right, he
puts all other religions in the shade:

> **'I am the way, and the truth, and the life. The only way
> to the Father is through me.'**

Peter understood what Jesus meant and preached it loud
and clear:

> **'Jesus is the only One who can save people. His name is
> the only power in the world that has been given to save
> people. We must be saved through him.'**

Paul preached the same message:

> **There is one God and one way human beings can reach
> God. That way is through Christ Jesus, who is himself
> human.**

What is the nearest religion to Christianity?

Judaism – the Jewish religion: it is half-way to Christianity.
Jews follow the Old Testament in:

- believing in the one God who chose Israel to be his
  people in the years before Christ.
- taking Saturday as their holy day.

Bible Bit

In the letter to the Hebrews an unknown writer explains to Jews who have become Christians how Jesus has made their old religion better, even perfect:

In the past God spoke to our ancestors through the prophets many times and in many different ways. But now in these last days God has spoken to us through his Son. God has chosen his Son to own all things, and through him he made the world. The Son reflects the glory of God and shows exactly what God is like. He holds everything together with his powerful word.

The law of Moses could not make anything perfect. But now a better hope has been given to us, and with this hope we can come near to God.

Every day the priests stand and do their religious service, often offering the same sacrifices. Those sacrifices can never take away sins. But after Christ offered one sacrifice for sins, forever, he sat down at the right side of God. And now Christ waits there for his enemies to be put under his power. With one sacrifice he made perfect forever those who are being made holy.

- eating only kosher food, chosen and prepared in line with God's instructions.

But this is only half-way to Christianity. Jews don't believe that:

- Jesus was and is the King that God promised.
- he has thrown God's Kingdom open to people of all races and countries.
- he shows us God in person and so has brought the earlier preparation stage to an end, making diet laws unnecessary.

- he has provided total forgiveness for everybody by dying in our place on the cross.
- he came back to life three days later to prove it (making Sunday an even better day to celebrate than Saturday).

Of course, there are different kinds of people calling themselves Jewish. The Jewish RACE is descended from God's people in the Old Testament. But not all these people are RELIGIOUS. Some don't believe in God at all.

Do pray for all Jewish people to come to know Jesus as the Messiah-King that God promised to their ancestors.

Is it OK to believe in evolution as a Christian?

I think it's quite OK to believe in evolution, but not in what I call 'Evolution with a capital E'.

'Evolution with a small e' is just the idea that the universe developed gradually from simple beginnings to its present shape. 'Evolution with a capital E' adds a second idea that the universe evolved BY ITSELF WITHOUT ANY HELP FROM GOD WHO – BY THE WAY – DOESN'T EXIST.

'Evolution with a small e' is just a scientific theory about how the world came to be the way it is. 'Evolution with a capital E' is a religious belief that tries to do away with God.

I'm not a scientist, so I have no idea whether evolution is true or not. I think most people imagine that it is more fully proved than it really is. But I have no problem as a Christian in believing it MAY be true.

Some people say evolution clashes with the beginning of the Bible, which gives its own version of how the universe began. But I see no clash. These are two views of the same thing from quite different angles.

What is this a description of? 'Mutual collision of the labial organs and inter-respiration with carbon dioxide.' Answer: two lovers kissing!

It's a perfectly accurate scientific description, but I don't think that the sentence 'I want our labial organs to collide and respirate each other with CO_2' will replace 'XXXXXXX' on Valentine cards. These are totally separate ways of looking at the same thing, suitable for quite different occasions and moods.

The Bible's version of how the world started is more like 'XXXXXXX'. It doesn't try to speak in scientific language at all, but gives us instead a simple God's-eye-view of what happened. And it tells us some vitally important facts that we wouldn't discover any other way:

1 God made the world – it didn't happen by accident.
2 He made the world in a well-planned order – it isn't a scatty jumble which might fall apart at any moment.
3 He gave the world a rhythm that helps the whole thing to keep going and growing. Day follows night into weeks and seasons.

When it says God made the whole universe in seven days, some people think this clashes with evolution's idea that it took millions of years. But the word 'day' doesn't always mean a single period of twenty-four hours. People sometimes talk about 'this day (and age)' to mean the time we're living in now. They may be thinking of a period lasting dozens of years, or even hundreds. More than this, we learn

---

Bible Bit

The Bible's record of how the world began parallels later scientific discovery:

Day 1 Light and dark, day and night
Day 2 Air and sky
Day 3 Water and land, plants and trees
Day 4 Sun, moon and stars
Day 5 Fish and birds
Day 6 Animals and human beings

from other parts of the Bible that 'one day' can mean the same as a thousand years or more to God (see Psalm 90:4; 2 Peter 3:8).

So perhaps evolution is discovering how God went about his work. The Bible calls each step a 'day' in God's week; but on our time-scale it may have been far longer than that.

Further ??? to think about by yourself or discuss with friends

1 Do you know someone who belongs to another religion? Do you think they really believe it for themselves, or is it just a family custom? What questions could you ask them to find out more about how their faith compares with Christianity?

2 What do Christianity and other faiths agree about? Are there things your Christian fellowship group could usefully do together with a group from another religion?

3 How might you answer a friend who says, 'All religions are the same'?

4 Which of your friends who isn't a Christian now do you think is most likely to become one? (They may belong to another religion at the moment, or have none at all.) What makes you think they might become a Christian? What could you do or say to help them?

5 If you have thought of any more questions for further discussion after reading this section, make a note of them here.

SEX

Why is it so important to be going out with someone?

There are several reasons, but some are better than others. The least good one is wanting to impress your friends. I know how vital it is to keep in with them and do things they respect. But when you go out with someone, you're building a special friendship with THAT ONE PERSON and getting to know them. They won't be very flattered if all the time you're more interested in what YOUR OTHER FRIENDS are going to think and say about your relationship.

A better reason is because it is the way God has made us. Somewhere in and around the teens a great change comes over us – well, several actually! But the one I'm thinking of affects who we like the look of.

I'm willing to bet you didn't feel great sexual attraction when you were, say, aged 7. Not if you were anything like 7-year-old Beryl who said, 'It's a pity you have to fall in love with boys because they always pinch you.' Or 6-year-old Norman who wrote, 'I wouldn't fall in love because girls are all spotty and they whisper.'

But suddenly all that goes out the window. The other sex start looking really rather nice, and some of them you definitely fancy. The idea of going out with one of them ALONE and being special to them is enough to send you into orbit!

This is all totally natural and normal. God has set our body-clock to make steps at different ages and stages towards being an adult. Going out with a friend from the

other sex is a first step towards finding a life-partner and getting married (which is God's plan for most – though not all – of us). We begin to learn how the other half ticks. How to build a friendship that will last more than a few days. How to take an interest in someone else and care about them.

This touches on the best reason of all, which may never have occurred to you. Forming a close friendship with someone of the other sex actually helps us to grow more like God! God said that he would make human beings to be like him. Not necessarily to LOOK like him – it doesn't mean God has one nose and two each of eyes, ears, arms and legs.

He said that we are like him in two ways in particular.

1 We share in his task of looking after the world and all its resources.
2 We are male and female.

Yes, I'll say it again. BEING MALE AND FEMALE MAKES US LIKE GOD. He is not a sexist male God. He has a big, loving, welcoming personality too great for any one human being to reflect. It takes a male and female together to show something of what God is like. God is all-over love and friendship and relationship. He is not a lonely 'myself and me alone'. He sometimes talks as 'we' and 'us', because he is a family of Father, Son and Holy Spirit. (For more about this, see 'Why does God have to be three people?' on page 11.) God's family-love naturally makes him want to create and make friends and share. It is that same instinct in us which makes us want a boyfriend or girlfriend of our own.

But remember, this is only a first step. Your first few

Bible Bit

Male and female is being like God:

> Then God said, 'And now we will make human beings; they will be like us and resemble us. They will have power over the fish, the birds, and all animals, domestic and wild, large and small.' So God created human beings, making them to be like himself. He created them male and female...

Paul learnt a great secret for living as a Christian. He reckoned that we should be happy no matter what's happening in our lives, and this includes whether we're going out with someone or not:

> I have learned to be satisfied with the things I have and with everything that happens. I know how to live when I am poor, and I know how to live when I have plenty. I have learned the secret of being happy at any time in everything that happens, when I have enough to eat and when I go hungry, when I have more than I need and when I do not have enough. I can do all things through Christ, because he gives me strength.

'going-out' friends may not last very long. The gaps in between may last longer than the friendships. It doesn't matter at all if you're not going out with someone at the moment, or if you haven't been out with anyone at all yet. There is loads of time, and plenty of other things God wants you to spend your time on.

How do you know when you're ready to have sex with someone?

Great question!

The answer most teachers and doctors give you is incredibly difficult and complicated. But God's answer is wonderfully simple and helpful.

People who think they know better than God will tell you something like this: 'You're ready to sleep with someone when you're sure you really know them and love them and trust them.'

Well, I hope that makes YOU clearer and happier, because it certainly doesn't do that for ME. How will I ever be SURE I really know or love or trust someone enough? My moods and feelings go up and down and in and out. I would be in bed with someone one day, but running off the next to find someone else.

In fact, if you let your feelings decide when you sleep with someone, you'll do it before you're ready. Most men have a very strong urge to sleep with the woman they fancy. They will soon kid themselves they REALLY know her and love her and trust her.

Most women have a very strong urge not to lose the man THEY fancy. So if he says he's ready to sleep with her, she will feel almost unbearable pressure to let him. If she didn't he might drop her for someone else.

Many young couples start having sex together before they are ready. It is the most private and intimate thing you can do. It means undressing in front of someone else and putting yourself completely into their arms. It means trusting they won't laugh at you or reject you. Often the relationship simply hasn't grown strong enough to carry the strain. Their bodies have done something more loving than they actually felt for each other. So they break up, but with far more pain than if they hadn't had sex together. They feel hurt and let down because they gave part of themselves to someone who no longer wants it.

And all the time God is longing to tell us his answer which will save all the heartache.

His answer is 'You're ready to sleep together when you've taken the step of marrying each other.' That's what sex really means. Two bodies join and become one to express two whole lives joining up and becoming a new family unit. If you have just promised to share all your money and belongings with somebody for the rest of your life, then of course you're ready to share your body with them as well. But not before. Unless and until you're prepared to get hitched, don't even think of having sex with someone else. It will only end in tears.

I'm so thankful God taught me not to sleep with girlfriends I had before I got married. My wife and I have only ever had sex with each other. We don't compare each other with earlier lovers. We have no painful or guilty memories. No worries about catching AIDS. Sex is a totally happy part of our lives. We would love you to have the same.

Bible Bit

God's guide to better and safer sex comes in the Garden of Eden:

> **So a man will leave his father and mother and be united with his wife, and the two will become one body.**
>
> **The man and his wife were naked, but they were not ashamed.**

Does God have ONE right person for you to marry?

Perhaps.

God has a plan mapped out for our lives as Christians (see Ephesians 2:10). He knows whether or not he wants us to marry at all. It is certainly his plan for most people, but it isn't a guaranteed right for anyone. So we have to stay open to the possibility that we may never get married.

This sounds an unhappy thought to many people. It may be because we have been brought up to think that getting married will automatically make us happy. It only will if it is God's plan for us. If he has actually designed us to enjoy our own company and work better alone, then getting married would make us very UNHAPPY.

So Christians need to keep praying, 'Lord, show me the right thing to do. Show me clearly how you want me to live' (Psalm 5:8). He may lead us to get married; or he may lead us to stay single. Whichever it is will be his gift to us at that time (see 1 Corinthians 7:7), and he will make us able to be happy with it.

Now, suppose for a moment God definitely does plan for you to get married. Has he got your future husband or wife already lined up? I think the answer is 'Yes, but…'

If you look at it from GOD'S point of view, he knows when you'll get married and who to. He will see to it that you meet each other – sooner or later the sparks will begin to fly – and, with his help, you should both live CHRISTIANLY ever after. I don't say 'HAPPILY ever after' because, in real life, there are tough times and problems. But in a Christian marriage there is a huge amount of happiness along the way. There's a true old saying: marriages are made in heaven. God has got the wedding date already booked in his diary.

But looking at it from OUR point of view, this is only half the story.

I actually found the idea that God had one right girl for me to marry quite worrying. How would I recognise her? Everyone told me God wouldn't switch on a halo round her head or play romantic music in my ears. So how could I tell which she was? Supposing I picked the wrong one?

The only guideline God seemed to give in the Bible was that a Christian should marry another Christian (see 1 Corinthians 7:39; 2 Corinthians 6:14–15). But this still left a pretty wide field. The churches I belonged to and the Christian holidays I helped to lead had loads of beautiful unmarried girls about the same age as me!

Then a friend told me to stop being stupid. He said, 'God has probably worked out what you're going to eat this evening. But if you go to a restaurant, you don't sit looking at the menu and praying, 'Lord, show me the right dish for me.' You choose something you like. And, if you're sensible, something that'll do you good. Same with a marriage partner. Find someone you like and who does you good.'

There is one big difference. You eat every day, so you can keep choosing different meals. But you only get married once. So make it a good choice. Wait till you meet someone who makes you want to marry them. Not just because they're dish, but because the more you get to know them the more you admire them and want to be part of their life. Because you both help each other to be better Christians.

When you meet someone like that, it is more than likely God is bringing you together. But if not, don't worry. As long as you keep following Jesus – praying to him and serving him – he will make it clear you're going the wrong way. Both my wife and I were engaged to other people first. But we both came to see fairly quickly that those engagements weren't working out. The relationships were breaking down instead of building up towards marriage.

It turned out a big help when Sue and I started going out with each other. This time we could see the difference. All the signs were positive, and God let us go ahead without stopping us.

Bible Bit

The story of how Adam met Eve is not your ordinary 'Mills and Boon' romance. But two things in their story are true of Christian marriages too. God brought them together:

> **The LORD God used the rib from the man to make a woman, and then he brought the woman to the man.**

Adam then had eyes only for Eve. He had a strong sense of 'We belong together – she's my other half!'

> **And the man said,**
> **'Now, this is someone whose bones came from my bones,**
> **whose body came from my body.'**

Is it OK for an unmarried couple to have a child?

Well, it's not illegal in this country.

And it's really good that children of unmarried parents don't get treated as second-class citizens any more. In my generation, they were called 'illegitimate'. This was grossly unfair because the children couldn't help what had happened. The PARENTS were illegitimate, not the children.

But having unmarried parents is not the start in life God would want for any child. Children need the total security of knowing their Mum and Dad will always be there for them. If their parents have married, they have clearly promised each other that they mean to stay together for ever. But if they haven't married, they have chosen for some reason not to make those promises. At least one of them must be holding back from giving a definite guarantee.

This is keeping your options open: like saying, 'Well yes, I'll probably play for Britain – but not if I get a better offer from France or the USA.' This sort of 'playing hard to get' is not good for the relationship, or for the children. Who knows when one of their parents might walk out?

This is why God says that sex and kids belong in the full security of marriage.

'Yes, but lots of married people get divorced.'

I know. My parents divorced and I was brought up in a lone-parent family. Four in every ten British marriages ends in divorce. That's 40 per cent, and it's 40 per cent too many.

Marriage doesn't come with an automatic guarantee that it will last forever. It needs hard work to keep it in good shape. But it's a whole lot safer than just living together. People who lived together before they married are twice as likely to get divorced as those who didn't. And people who live together without ever getting married are more likely still to separate.

Sadly, a lot of young people are the children of these broken relationships. If you are one, I can share a bit of the hurt with you because I was too. But the great news is, God is the perfect parent. He can look after us when our human parents fail, and he can make up to us for the things we miss out on. He doesn't leave us losing out for the rest of our lives.

As a child on my own I really wanted a brother. It was my number one prayer to God. But without a dad I couldn't see how this would happen. When I was 8, I had to go into hospital for an operation. One of the doctors said, 'Tell your mum to come in here, and we'll give her a brother for you'. It didn't sound quite right as an answer to prayer (I'm STILL not sure what he meant!) and I was much too embarrassed to pass the message on. So it was back to prayer.

Then, when I became a Christian, I discovered that God had given me hundreds and thousands of brothers (and sisters!) in HIS family. I meet new ones almost every week. The friendship of other Christians is one of the things I enjoy most in life.

Is it wrong to get divorced?

People asked Jesus much the same question (see Matthew 19:3–9). He said that divorce certainly is wrong in God's sight: 'God has joined the two together, so no one should separate them.' But, in the Old Testament, Moses had allowed people to divorce. When Jesus was asked why, he replied, 'Moses allowed you to divorce your wives because you refused to accept God's teaching, but divorce was not allowed in the beginning.'

This draws a helpful dividing line between those who follow God's teaching and those who don't. God invented marriage and he meant it to be for keeps. However, he understands that people who don't believe in him or pray for his help may find it too hard to live with the same person for the whole of their lives. He doesn't want them to divorce or break their promises but, with great sadness, he accepts that it will sometimes happen. Divorce is always painful, especially for any children; but it may in the end be less painful than continuing to live with someone you don't like any more.

So I think the law of the land is right to allow divorce and, at the same time, right to make people wait and see a counsellor first, in case their marriage can be saved. This is always better than divorce.

Sadly, some Christians get divorced too, but I don't think it need ever come to this. Christians do try to follow God's teaching, so we agree to marry another Christian who wants to please and serve Jesus too. We believe that God will lead us to the marriage partner he has planned and prepared for us. In our case, therefore, it should be completely true that 'God has joined the two together'. He is then with us to help us learn how to follow his teaching in our new life and home together. His Spirit gradually makes us less selfish and more like Jesus. He is ready to help us sort out any problems or disagreements. We just need to be humble enough to ask him.

A Christian marriage that works well is a taste of heaven on earth. We would be mad to let anything spoil it.

When Billy Graham, the American preacher, was leading a mission in Britain some years ago, the *Observer* newspaper interviewed the other members of his team. It is unusual enough for an English newspaper to give any Christians a good press, let alone American missionaries who come over here to make converts. Yet the journalist had to admit he liked and even admired them. He ended his article with the words, 'And not even one unhappy marriage amongst them.'

Bible Bit

Jesus has such a high view of marriage that, even if you separate or divorce, he thinks of you as still married:

> 'I tell you that anyone who divorces his wife and marries another woman is guilty of adultery (ie breaking his marriage promises).'

What about women whose husbands are violent?

I certainly wouldn't want to condemn any woman, perhaps with children, to live in a home where she's afraid that her husband will batter and abuse her. (Or sometimes it is a man with a violent wife.) But I would still be terribly sad if it came to divorce. I look on that as the very last answer, after everything else to change the situation has been tried.

First, the couple could try to get counselling help. Why is one partner violent? Let's see if we can help to solve that problem. Is he or she drinking too much because of money or job worries? Is the other perhaps making things worse by nagging or (just as common) ignoring their spouse?

Perhaps the couple need to separate for a while to let things cool down. If there are other family members involved, they might help. And, if the couple are Christians or friendly with a church, here is a second family they could turn to for support. Let's get people praying for them, even if they won't pray themselves. God loves to answer prayer. And to mend damaged marriages.

Should a married person who has an affair with someone else get divorced?

It depends on the person who has NOT had the affair. If the faithful partner wants a divorce, it is their right. This is the one reason Jesus allows for getting a divorce. If your partner has an affair, he or she is breaking their marriage promise and so breaking the marriage.

However, you don't HAVE to get a divorce. If the faithful partner can forgive and work to build the marriage again, that will be better.

One other thing needs to be clear. If they do get divorced, the unfaithful partner is not then free in God's sight to marry the person they had the affair with. God treasures and protects the first marriage, hoping the couple will get back together.

Marriage is one of God's most precious gifts. He expects us to treat it as far more valuable than even the biggest win on the lottery. Let's pray we can live up to his high hopes for us.

What is the Christian attitude towards homosexual people?

Somewhere in and around the teens, most of us change our minds about the other sex. They used to seem boring or a pain, but suddenly they become definitely the most interesting species in the animal kingdom! Most people manage this gear-change from reverse to fast forward in one easy move.

However, some need to warm up gradually. They go through a phase where they fancy someone of their own sex before they can switch those feelings to the other sex. The scientific word for these feelings is 'homosexual', which means 'attracted to your own sex'. Most people now use the nicer, shorter word 'gay' for these feelings (and sometimes the term 'lesbian' for a girl who loves another girl).

This gay phase is often a form of admiration, a longing to be like the person they are looking up to. It usually lasts only a few weeks or months and is a natural step towards straight sex feelings.

A few, perhaps 2 or 3 per cent – that is, on average one person in a full-size school class – get stuck and find they can't develop normal feelings. They go on fancying their own sex for years.

Why does this happen? There has been a lot of talk about a 'gay gene' which makes gay people have a differently shaped brain. The press loves to report sensational new ideas like this, but most scientists are very far from agreeing the research is proved (see **Note** on page 80).

I think gay feelings are much more likely to be caused by family problems. What can often happen is this. Someone suffers a breakdown early in life in the relationship with their parent of the same sex – a girl with her mum, a boy with his dad. Maybe the parent dies, or leaves home, or abuses them, or gives all their love to someone else in the family. This leaves the child growing up without the love from their same-sex parent which we all need if we are to develop normally.

This is exactly what happened to me. My parents divorced when I was one, and my dad walked out of our lives. When my sexual feelings awakened in my teens, I fancied other boys because (without realising it) I was looking for the father-love I had missed all those years.

So gay feelings aren't the gay person's fault. Christians should NEVER bully them or make fun of them or call them 'poofter' or 'pervert'. Jesus expects us to care about them and be kind to them, just as we should to everyone else (see Mark 12:31). Like anyone with family problems, they need good friends to give them the support and company they're not getting at home.

Bible Bit

God's design for reproducing the human race is straight sex:

> God created human beings, making them to be like himself. He created them male and female, blessed them, and said, 'Have many children...'

Can you be a practising gay or lesbian and a true Christian?

Obviously, gay people can't help the way they feel. But they can control what they do about those feelings. You can't help birds flying over your head, but you can stop them building nests in your hair. Just because you fancy someone the same sex as you, you don't have to have sex with them or even go out with them. Christians definitely shouldn't. God doesn't want people to have gay sex; he even says he hates it (see Leviticus 18:22). But this doesn't mean he hates THEM – he loves them.

When I was 7, my mum caught me nicking money from her purse to buy ice-lollies from the corner shop. She wasn't pleased. She hated what I'd done, but she still loved me. And, because she loved me, she was much more worried about what the act of stealing would do to me than she was about the waste of money. (In her concern to reform my criminal tendencies, she took me to the local church's family service and set me on the road to becoming a Christian – but that's another story!)

It's the same with God. He doesn't like gay sex because it cheats people of the beauty and happiness of straight sex, which is what he designed us for. Anyone can see that a man's body fits a woman's, not another man's, and the same the other way round with a woman's! This is just the outside casing of the way he has made us all through. It takes one man plus one woman to make a new family, which is God's way of producing children and guiding the human race into its next generation. It is his way of making most of us happy and secure.

God wants to help people through the gay stage they are in now to become straight. He can do this through the love

Bible Bit

Paul says God doesn't want gay sex happening in his kingdom, and he can help them not to be gay any more:

> Those who live immoral lives, who are idol worshippers, adulterers or homosexuals – will have no share in his (God's) kingdom. Neither will thieves or greedy people, drunkards, slanderers or robbers. There was a time when some of you were just like that but now your sins are washed away, and you are set apart for God, and he has accepted you because of what the Lord Jesus Christ and the Spirit of our God have done for you.

and prayers of the church family they belong to, and some-times the help of a specialist. I know he can because that's how it was with me. My feelings were gay till I was in my 20s, but God heard my prayers and gradually straightened me out. Now I'm married with two children in their teens, and I've never been happier.

Should gay people have the right to get married and have sex together?

Sadly (in my opinion), some gay people are comfortable as they are and don't want to change; or they give up waiting and think they never will change. We can't force them. The law of the land allows two partners of the same sex to live together in a steady relationship. I think it is good they have that freedom, but God wants something better for them. I hope Christians won't settle for less than what God wants.

And I wouldn't call a gay partnership a marriage or start it with a gay wedding. Marriages are meant to last for the rest of our lives; but gay people can (and, I believe, should) look forward to becoming straight. God designed marriage to be straight, not gay. The first married couple were Adam and Eve, not Adam and Eric!

What about gay people who try to become straight, but don't?

They shouldn't stop trying – things are a lot more hopeful now than in the past. But they need to remember three things.

1 They really need to want to change.

Anyone who is basically happy to be gay will stay gay.

2 The change is unlikely to be a sudden miracle.

If the gay feelings are very deep-rooted, the probable cause was the loss of a good relationship with their same-sex parent. The cure is in finding that parent-love in one or more older people of the same sex. Sometimes this is a professional counsellor, sometimes it is through people like leaders of a youth group at church. This can often take years to build up (and make up for the years of loss). The change happens slowly and gradually over this time.

3 All forms of healing come from God, but he doesn't treat everyone the same way and we often don't understand what he does.

Some people he heals very quickly, with little or no prayer; others he heals much more slowly, after months or years of praying; some may never recover completely in this life, but have to wait for his total healing in heaven. We need to build up the incredible sort of trust Job had in God, when he said, 'Even if God kills me, I have hope in him' (Job 13:15; for reasons why God sometimes doesn't answer our prayers see 'Does God always hear you when you pray?' on page 17).

If you have an abortion, some people say you have taken a life. Will you still go to heaven?

We don't go to heaven because we have been good: only because we have asked God to forgive us for being bad, and he has (see 'Does absolutely every non-Christian go to hell?' on page 105). The incredible good news from Jesus is that even murderers can go to heaven, provided they admit they have done wrong and ask to be forgiven. However, the question here is whether abortion itself is right or wrong. Is it taking a human life?

Many people will try to tell you that a baby only becomes a person when she or he is born. There is no evidence to support this at all. Genetically, the new person is a mini-human being as soon as their dad's sperm has fertilised their mum's egg. They simply grow and develop from that moment on. There is no later stage when 'it' magically turns into 'her' or 'him'.

The Bible seems to say the same. King David believed that God supervises the nine months while a baby takes shape in a mother's womb (Psalm 139:13–16). So ending someone's life before they are born is killing them. Some people like to wrap this in scientific-sounding language like 'aborting the foetus' or 'terminating the pregnancy' to make it sound less bad. But, in fact, it is murder, and a gruesome form of murder because the victim is totally defenceless.

The law of the land allows abortion early in pregnancy if:

1 the mother's life is at risk;
2 her health is at risk;
3 the health of any older sisters or brothers is at risk;
4 the baby is likely to be handicapped.

In my view, this is allowing more abortions than it should. I think the first example, where the mother might die, is the only one where you can say an abortion might be right or the less bad thing to do. It is extremely rare, but does happen occasionally. In that case, I think we probably should use an abortion to save the mother, and leave the unborn child in God's care (see 'Do you go to heaven or hell if you die when you're a baby?' on page 109).

The second and third cases, where the mother or any other children might suffer ill-health if the baby is born, are also extremely rare. And I can't see that they would ever make it right to kill someone, especially when medicine and loving care can do so much to help people who are ill and even cure them.

The fourth case, where the baby is likely to be handicapped, is more common, but who are we to deny that person the right to life? Only God has the right to bring life to an end, and he has designed our reproductive system so that many handicapped foetuses do abort themselves or 'miscarry' before birth. If they do make it all the way to being born, surely God wants them to have a life on earth like the rest of us.

People say, 'It must be a dreadful life for them. They'd be better off dead.' But how do we know? I fear it is often a cover-up. What we mean is 'We don't want the trouble and pain of looking after them.' But many who have worked with handicapped people, or brought them up, will tell you that they bring more joy than sadness. And they help us to become kinder and more caring people.

Bible Bit

Job understands that God is in charge of life and death. When his children are tragically killed, he says:

> 'I was born with nothing, and I will die with nothing. The LORD gave, and now he has taken away.'

David understands that God is in charge of our life before birth:

> You made my whole being;
>   you formed me in my mother's body...
> You saw my bones being formed
>   as I took shape in my mother's body.
> When I was put together there,
>   you saw my body as it was formed.

'Hasn't a woman the right to decide what happens to her own body?'

Not if this means killing another person. Once a baby has been conceived, the mother's body is not hers alone. She is housing another human being. She has no more right to murder that inmate than she would have the right to kill someone staying in her house.

Except in the rare case of rape, the mother chose to have sex with the baby's father. They may not have meant to have a baby. They may have tried to prevent it by using a contraceptive. But they knew that no contraceptive is 100

71

per cent safe. If you have sex, you give away your 'right' to be childless. It's the risk you take.

'Surely it's cruel to bring an unwanted baby into the world.'

Who says that a baby is unwanted?

Even if the baby was UNPLANNED, the parents (especially the mum) often grow to want it very much as the pregnancy goes on. My daughter was conceived even though we were using birth control. To begin with, we didn't want a baby: we were afraid that my wife would lose her job. But the nine months of gradual development changed our minds completely. By the time she was born, we had decided to call her Joy because that was how we had come to feel about her. I love her now even more than I did then. Nobody suggested an abortion when she was first conceived: but if they had, the terrifying thought is I might have agreed to it. Now I know what a lovely, gifted person I would have killed. It gives me a cold sweat to think about it. No wonder I want the law against abortion tightened up.

Sometimes the baby's own family have got problems which make them unable to look after a new member properly. But even if they don't want the child, it is quite wrong to call her or him UNWANTED. There are many couples unable to have babies of their own who long to adopt a child like this. There simply aren't enough so-called 'unwanted' babies to go round.

If you rape someone, will God forgive you?

Jesus died on the cross for EVERY wrong thing done by EVERY member of the human race EVER. This means God can forgive even the most revolting crimes.

He would even forgive you raping someone IF you:

- turn away from what you have done and admit that it was wrong;

- tell God what you have done and ask him to forgive you;
- ask for his strength never to do it again;
- say sorry to the person you raped and offer to help put right the damage you have done them.

Rape is almost as bad as murder – some people would say worse. It is forcing someone to have sex with you when they don't want to. Sometimes it involves violence. One or more people take a struggling victim; hold them down or threaten them with a knife; strip their clothes off; and attack their private parts.

Sometimes there is no physical violence at all. Instead there is emotional pressure. A girl and boy go out for the evening. One expects the other to end up in bed. He or she may not even ask, just make it clear that's what they want. (It is usually men who rape women, but not always: there are women who seduce men against their will.) And if this person is the stronger character, the other partner may not know how to say no. They may be frightened of a row or a fight – or of losing the friendship.

In both cases, the two bodies join in the way that God had designed to be the most loving cuddle between a man and woman, but here one of the pair feels nothing but shock, hate, pain, shame and fear. Depending on the person, these feelings may take weeks, years or even the rest of their life to get over.

How could anyone – how could you – do such a thing? The answer is, all too easily, if you pay no attention to the warnings all round you.

The twentieth century is sex-mad. Practically all love films think they have got to show the couple in bed together. Porno mags and videos are easy to get hold of. People paper their walls with pictures of nudes. It is all blaring out a simple message: sex is the most important thing in life; sex is what we're all about. This is an enormously powerful message, and it doesn't take much to persuade us. Once we believe it, we think that other people are there to feed our sexual hunger. If they don't want to, we'll find a way to make them.

Christians need to understand this is the pressure on them, and they need to ask God's help to stand against it. Rape and the cheap view of sex that leads down to it are the last thing God wants. They make him sick and make him cry.

His message is quite different. HE is the most important thing in life. Learning to love him and follow him is what we're all about. In his game-plan, sex plays the lovely waiting game. It is the instinct which leads us to look for a life-partner, but it only comes out into the open when we have found that person. Then two people give each other the best present they have got – themselves! For ever! Their two lives become one, with no trickery, no force, no violence, no rape. Just love and trust and peace.

If you have been abused for years and you kill the person who was abusing you, is that right or wrong?

Abusing a child or young person is a terrible thing. It takes advantage of someone not old enough or strong enough or clever enough to defend themselves. It can be very frightening for them. It can leave them unable to trust anyone. It can make them hate the abuser and – even worse but more likely – hate themselves. They imagine there is something cheap or dirty about them which made the abuser treat them so badly.

Worst of all, the young victim will probably lose faith in God. How could a loving God allow it to happen?

God is still there. He is close to his people when they suffer and he feels their pain (see Isaiah 63:9, 'When they suffered, he suffered also'). And he is very angry indeed. He doesn't step in and prevent the abuse in the first place, because he has made human beings terrifyingly free to do what they want; BUT HE HOLDS THEM RESPONSIBLE FOR WHAT THEY DO. He will certainly punish child-abusers in the next life if not before.

He may also use our human forces of law to catch, arrest and imprison. But he doesn't want the abused person to take the law into their own hands and kill their tormentor. Murder is always wrong, however bad the abuse (see Exodus 20:13). Two wrongs never make a right.

What if you kill someone in self-defence?

This is the difference between murder and 'manslaughter' (or personslaughter?). Murder is when you kill someone on purpose. Manslaughter is when you kill them without meaning to, either completely by accident (like a car crash) or when you are afraid they may kill you if you don't fight back (like in war).

The law of the land punishes manslaughter much less heavily than murder, if at all. And God's law is just the same (see Exodus 22:4; 1 Kings 2:5–6).

However, God doesn't want anyone killed, not even child-abusers. He would rather not have to punish them. Anyone who abuses children or young people has got BIG problems. God wants to help them sort those problems out. Then they will be ready to ask forgiveness from him and from the people they have abused. They will be willing to do anything they can to put right the damage they have caused. This is much the best solution to the crime of abuse. Do pray for it to happen.

If you have suffered any form of physical or sexual abuse yourself, you may be glad of the help offered through the **Helpline** on page 127.

Shouldn't people with AIDS have the same rights?

Yes, of course. They are human beings and citizens of the country they belong to, so they should have the same rights – and duties – as anyone else. In the areas of life the law can control, they do have the same rights: the right to a doctor and hospital when they are ill; the right not to be taxed any more than other people; freedom from being arrested unless it looks as if they have committed a crime.

However, there are areas of life where the law can't easily protect you. This is where some people who are known to have AIDS, or the HIV virus that is thought to lead to it, have suffered. They are forced to have frequent health-checks. They have found it hard to get a job. Landlords have turned them out of their homes. The amount they have to pay in insurance has gone up. Old friends, even

Bible Bit

Here is a typical story of Jesus meeting someone other people hated and despised (you can find it in Luke 19:1–10). Imagine that Zacchaeus had AIDS. Would Jesus react any differently? What about you?

> Jesus was going through the city of Jericho. A man was there named Zacchaeus, who was a very important tax collector, and he was wealthy. He wanted to see who Jesus was, but he was not able because he was too short to see above the crowd. He ran ahead to a place where Jesus would come, and he climbed a sycamore tree so he could see him. When Jesus came to that place, he looked up and said to him, 'Zacchaeus, hurry and come down! I must stay at your house today.'
>
> Zacchaeus came down quickly and welcomed him gladly. All the people saw this and began to complain, 'Jesus is staying with a sinner!'
>
> But Zacchaeus stood and said to the Lord, 'I will give half of my possessions to the poor. And if I have cheated anyone, I will pay back four times more.'
>
> Jesus said to him, 'Salvation has come to this house today, because this man also belongs to the family of Abraham. The Son of Man came to find lost people and save them.'

their own families, have stopped wanting to know them.

These are dreadful things which shouldn't happen, but you can understand why they do. Many people are frightened of catching the disease themselves. Or they don't know what to say to someone who is dying. Or they can't afford to offer their services to someone who won't be around long to pay for them.

There are many groups and organisations trying to improve attitudes towards people with AIDS. There is one group that should be showing the way – the Christian

Church. Its founder was famous for caring about the outcasts of his day, the people no one else would touch – people like prostitutes, tax-collectors for the hated foreign government that ruled their country, and people who had caught the dreaded skin-disease called leprosy.

Jesus told his followers to cure the sick and care for them (see Matthew 10:8; 25:34–40), so here is an extra right that people with AIDS can expect – the right to have Christians praying for them and caring about them. Their Christian friends shouldn't desert them but should go on being friends. Other Christians who don't know them should support charities that are trying to make things easier for them. (You can find some addresses in the **Helpline** on page 127.)

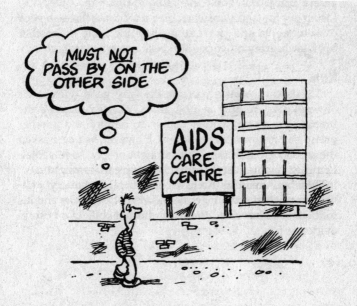

Further ??? to think about by yourself or discuss with friends

1 What things do you like best in God's instructions about sex? What do you find harder to take on board?

2 What could you say to a friend who says, 'The Bible's teaching about sex is out of date'?

3 Do you know any friends who are hurting because of abuse or divorce in the family? What can you do to help?

4 If God was sitting talking to you, what questions would you like to ask him about sex?

Try writing them down on a piece of paper. Then give it to him as a 'burnt offering'. Set fire to the piece of paper in a safe place! But don't then forget about the questions. Listen out for God's answers: they may come through your own thoughts and prayers, reading the Bible or another book, or hearing other people speak about the subject.

Note

The leading spokesman for the 'gay gene' idea is Dr Simon LeVay, writing in 1991 and 1993. He compared the brains of a group of men known to be gay and another group he presumed were straight. However, he never asked the second group if they were straight or gay; so it is totally misleading to treat their brains as typical of straight men. In 1993 the American 'Archives of General Psychiatry' published an article reviewing the theories of Dr LeVay and his followers, and decided that they did not contain any solid evidence.

THINGS YOU CAN HAVE TOO MUCH OF!

How much is too much?

Jesus never laid down exact amounts, like 'Never drink more than one can of lager at a time' or 'The most spending money you should ever have on you is £100.' A good thing too, because different people can take different amounts of drink, and the value of money changes over the years.

He just stated one simple truth: 'No one can serve two masters … You cannot serve both God and worldly riches' (see Matthew 6:24). You've got too much money when you start serving it instead of God; when you spend all your time wanting money, dreaming about it, talking about it, thinking how to make it and spend it. Jesus spoke a lot about money and possessions, but his words are equally true of drink or other legal drugs. You've had too much of THEM when you become hooked on them; when you become their slave, instead of God's slave.

To show what he meant, Jesus told a story about a rich businessman who owned more land and crops and barns than he knew what to do with (you can find it in Luke 12:18–21; these verses are from the *Good News* Bible):

(The rich man said) 'I will say to myself, Lucky man! You have all the good things you need for many years. Take life easy, eat, drink, and enjoy yourself!' But God said to him, 'You fool! This very night you will have to give up your life; then who will get all these things you have kept for yourself?'

And Jesus concluded, 'This is how it is with those who pile up riches for themselves but are not rich in God's sight.'

If God told you that you were going to heaven tonight, leaving behind all your money and everything else you own, would you mind? If you do, then these things have probably got too much of a hold on you.

This is all quite easy to understand, but it takes a lifetime of working out from day to day to become completely free of wanting too much.

Bible Bit

More of what Jesus said:

'Don't store treasures for yourselves here on earth, where moths and rust will destroy them and thieves can break in and steal them. But store your treasures in heaven, where they cannot be destroyed by moths or rust and where thieves cannot break in and steal them. Your heart will be where your treasure is.'

Can't money make you happy?

Not if you spend it all on yourself. The National Lottery publicity plays on the idea that you would be over the moon if 'it could be you'. In fact, there have been press reports of some of the biggest winners falling out with their families and hiding away in misery. This is partly because they have been harassed by people demanding their share of the winnings; and partly because, when they actually got it, they had no idea how to handle such a huge amount of money. The worries and pressures money brings are no fun at all. I wouldn't advise anyone to play the lottery: it brings sadness all round. Not only to the tiny number of big winners, but to the vast majority who lose money on it.

Yet there is one way that money can make you very happy indeed. Give it away!

Advice to big earners
(Even to lottery winners, though, of course, that won't include any readers of this book!)

Keep what you really need to live on and look after your family, then give the rest away as presents to people who need it: to charities helping the poor, and especially to churches and missions bringing the good news of Jesus to people who aren't yet Christians.

Then some people will be in heaven, thanks to the money you gave. This will give you – and them – a real thrill. And it will give God the biggest thrill of all.

If you have worked hard and earned lots of money, shouldn't you enjoy spending it without feeling bad?

Yes, as long as you don't squeeze God out of the picture.

For one thing, I reckon he deserves some thanks. Who made you able to work hard? At a job that's so well paid? And brought you up in a part of the world where there are so many enjoyable things to buy?

But more than that – if you're a Christian, who does the money really belong to? Following Jesus means putting him in charge of everything we have and everything we do, and this includes how we spend our money.

You could make a list of all the things you would like to buy over the next few months. Then take the risk of asking God to show you which ones he wants you to get and which he doesn't. He may make you uneasy about things

Bible Bit

A wise prayer:

> Don't make me either rich or poor;
> just give me enough food for each day.

Paul explains how dangerous money can be:

> Those who want to become rich bring temptation to
> themselves and are caught in a trap. They want many
> foolish and harmful things that ruin and destroy people.
> The love of money causes all kinds of evil. Some people
> have left the faith, because they wanted to get more
> money, but they have caused themselves much sorrow.

If we find we have more than we need, Paul and Timothy
have this advice for giving:

> You should each give, then, as you have decided, not
> with regret or out of a sense of duty; for God loves the
> one who gives gladly. And God is able to give you more
> than you need, so that you will always have all you
> need for yourselves and more than enough for every
> good cause.

you only want because your friends have got them or that
are way over the top when you remember how people in
other parts of the world have got so little.

For the rest of the things on your list, God knows what
you need and he wants you to enjoy them. So you can feel
really good about buying them.

If you have got it right, there should be some money left
over. Don't spend it all on your needs. Even if there is not very
much, give some of it back to God as a thank-you present.

Advice for students and other low earners

In the Old Testament, God told his people to give at least 10
per cent of their produce to support his work. People who

can afford more should give more. But 10 pence in every £1 sounds a good guideline to me for all of us. I suggest you give some to your church; some to a project in a developing country which your school is supporting; or some to a missionary society helping people to hear about Jesus.

Bible Bit

When God's people gave their valuables to help pay for building the temple, David prayed:

> **These things did not really come from me and my people.**
> **Everything comes from you;**
> **we have given you back what you gave us.**

Paul tells his helper, Timothy, how to instruct Christians who are well off in how they should treat their money:

> **Command those who are rich with things of this world not to be proud. Tell them to hope in God, not in their uncertain riches. God richly gives us everything to enjoy. Tell the rich people to do good, to be rich in doing good deeds, to be generous and ready to share.**

If you take drugs, will you still go to heaven?

Once you have started following Jesus, he promises to see you safe to heaven (see **Note** on page 92). There's no single wrong thing you may do – like taking illegal drugs – that will make him change his mind.

This doesn't make doing the wrong thing right. Nor does it mean that Jesus thinks it's OK to do something wrong. The question here is 'Is it wrong for a Christian to take drugs? Does Jesus think it's OK or not?'

Let's be clear, first of all, what we mean by drugs. We're talking about drugs that are illegal unless prescribed by a doctor. There are two common legal drugs – alcohol and tobacco – which have their own questions later (pages 89–91).

Illegal drugs have been banned for two good reasons:

1 They are dangerous.

There may be times when our bodies and minds aren't working properly and we need drugs as pain-killers or sleeping pills. But if we take them when we are well, they can badly affect our reactions or judgement. 'Stimulants', like pep pills, speed us up. 'Depressants', like cannabis (once you've got used to it), slow us down. 'Hallucinogens', like LSD, give us fantasies. All this is bad enough if you are just walking to school or doing your homework. It becomes a real danger if you're crossing the road or cycling or swimming or handling a machine.

2 They are addictive.

Our system soon comes to rely on drugs and won't work so well without them. We begin to feel we need them, like alcoholics need to keep drinking. What's more, the effect wears off faster so we need bigger and bigger doses.

There is no way Jesus wants us to damage ourselves like this. He wants us to enjoy life at its best, not live this sort of half-life. He can help us see through the reasons why some people fall for drugs in the first place.

'It'll give you a high'

Sure, some drugs give you a great feeling for a little while, but they let you down with a bump afterwards. Through his Holy Spirit in our lives, Jesus opens us up to the feelings God wants us to experience.

'It'll help you forget'

Some people have sad problems to face at home or school, and some drugs can soothe the pain and make you sleepy. But Jesus wants to give us the strength and wisdom to face our problems and deal with them, not run away from them.

'Everyone's doing it'

In most schools there are groups or gangs who think it's cool to take drugs. If you're friends with them, it can be really hard to say no. But you're also friends with Jesus; and there are some things his friends have got to say 'No' to. He'll help us to do it. It's rubbish to say EVERYONE'S taking drugs; only a very small number of people do. But even if everyone else did, it would be no good reason for you to

Bible Bit

Jesus wants to give us the best in life and protect us from harm:

> 'A thief comes to steal and kill and destroy, but I came to give life – life in all its fullness.'

Paul tells us that our bodies belong to God, so we must not damage or abuse them:

> You should know that your body is a temple for the Holy Spirit who is in you. You have received the Holy Spirit from God. So you do not belong to yourselves, because you were bought by God for a price. So honour God with your bodies.

do the same. After all, everyone's selfish and proud, but being selfish and proud are still wrong. Christians are in the business of learning how to turn selfishness and pride out of their lives. In the same way, God will teach us to say no to illegal drugs.

The first time you try heroin, do you get addicted?

Not automatically, and if you could be sure you could take just one shot, you probably wouldn't be hooked.

The trouble is that if you reach the point of agreeing to take heroin at all, you're probably in the mood to take it again and again. That's when you WILL get hooked.

Don't forget, using heroin is against the law, so you would have to take it in hiding. Unless you knew how to inject yourself, someone else would be injecting it into you with a needle that might be diseased. To take those risks, I think you would have to be pretty desperate. I doubt if you would have the will power to say, 'Once and once only.'

Very few people try heroin as their first drug. They usually reach it by stages, using other drugs that get steadily harder and stronger. They are already addicted to the drug habit by the time they get to heroin, so they have next to no chance of avoiding heroin addiction.

Heroin is a destroyer. Don't just take my word for it. Read this 'Psalm of Heroin Addiction' written by an addict:

King Heroin is my shepherd, I shall always want.
He makes me lie down in the gutters;
  He leads me beside the troubled waters;
He destroys my soul.
He leads me in the paths of wickedness for the effort's
  sake.
Yes, I shall walk through the valley of poverty and will
  fear all evil,
For you, Heroin, are with me.

> Your needle and capsule try to comfort me;
> You strip the table of groceries in the presence of my
> family;
> You rob my head of all reason.
> My cup of sorrow runs over.
> Surely heroin addiction will stalk me all the days of my
> life,
> And I will dwell in the house of the damned forever.

A policeman found this sad version of Psalm 23 in a phone box. On the back was written: 'Truly this is my psalm. I am a young woman, 20 years of age, and for the past year and a half I have been wandering down the nightmare alley of the junkies. I want to stop taking dope and I try but I can't. Jail didn't cure me. Nor did hospitalisation help me for long.

'The doctor told my family it would have been better and indeed kinder if the person who first got me hooked on dope had taken a gun and blown my brains out, and I wish to God she had. My God, how I do wish it' (quoted in *Dare to Discipline* by James Dobson, Kingsway, 1988 edition, pp199–200; I've put the words into modern language).

Pray for desperate people in situations like this. And make sure you never reach that state yourself.

There is only one way to avoid heroin addiction. Never start taking drugs in the first place. ANY drugs.

What about smoking?

I can't think of one thing to say in favour of smoking. When I was a child and in my teens, I kept trying to help my mum give up. She wanted to stop but she couldn't. She was completely addicted. She finally died of a heart attack at least ten years younger than her sisters who don't smoke.

Smoking isn't illegal, but I wouldn't mind if it was. It pollutes the atmosphere, wastes money, makes you ill and can even kill you. I find it hard to believe this is what God had in mind when he invented tobacco.

People say it calms their nerves, but I find prayer much better for that. And prayer doesn't damage your health!

As for the idea that smoking makes you look mature – what is so mature about sucking a burning tube and breathing out a nasty smell on everyone else?!

It is much more mature to say 'No, thanks'. REAL MEN – AND WOMEN – DON'T SMOKE.

Is it wrong to drink alcohol?

No – unlike smoking, I don't think drinking is wrong. Here is one drug – and caffeine is perhaps another – that God seems to have made for fairly general use. Jesus must have liked it: he provided extra wine for a wedding; and he told his followers to use a glass of wine as a way of remembering him dying for us on the cross (see John 2:1–11; Matthew 26:27–29).

What is wrong is when we misuse God's gifts to us. Sleeping pills aren't wrong when we need them; only when we don't. In the same sort of way, it isn't wrong to drink, but it is wrong to get drunk; worse still, to get addicted to the stuff and become an alcoholic.

The trouble is that alcohol is habit-forming. One glass of wine or a half-pint of beer every now and then is quite safe. But if you're with friends you want to impress, or if you're feeling depressed, it is all too easy to have another round, and another, and another.

Drinking too much is no joke. It can kill you – damaging liver, heart and brain. And if you mix it into that deadliest cocktail, drinking 'n' driving, it makes you a killer. Much better to drink no alcohol at all than to get trapped under its influence.

Anyway, most strong drink is what they call 'an acquired taste': something you may like when you're older, but yucky the first time you drink it. Why not wait till you like it? Actually choosing to drink something you don't really like sounds pretty dumb to me.

It is also quite wrong to think we need alcohol to make us cheerful and good fun to be with. God can do that

Bible Bit

The psalm-writer sings to God:

> You (God) make the grass for cattle
> and vegetables for the people.
> You make food grow from the earth.
> You give us wine that makes happy hearts
> and olive oil that makes our faces shine.
> You give us bread that gives us strength.

Wise advice from King Solomon:

> Drinking too much makes you loud and foolish. It's stupid to get drunk.

According to Paul, it is even worse than stupid to make a habit of getting drunk:

> Surely you know that the people who do wrong will not inherit God's kingdom. Do not be fooled. Those who sin sexually, worship idols, take part in adultery, those who are male prostitutes or men who have sexual relations with other men, those who steal, are greedy, get drunk, lie about others or rob – these people will not inherit God's kingdom.

himself! The New Testament tells us to fill up with the Holy Spirit, not alcoholic spirits (see Ephesians 5:18).

PS One other wrong thing – it's against the law to buy alcohol before you're 18. And God wants Christians to keep the law (see Romans 13:1).

Further ??? to think about by yourself or discuss with friends

1 What do you think Jesus meant when he told us to store our treasures in heaven?

2 How can you work out a reasonable amount for pocket money or an allowance?

3 Why do people want to take drugs, or smoke, or drink under-age?

4 If Jesus was sitting talking with you, what do you think he might say to people who take drugs, or smoke, or drink under-age? Write your ideas in the space below.

What might he want to say to you?

What would you want to ask or say to him?

Note

See John 10:27–29, where Jesus says, 'No one can steal them out of my hand.' At first sight, Hebrews 6:4–6 seems to go against this when it says, 'Some people cannot be brought back again to a changed life. They were once in God's light, and enjoyed heaven's gift, and shared in the Holy Spirit ... But they fell away from Christ.' This isn't talking about a single bad deed but a definite turning away from Jesus after starting to follow him. No one else and no other thing we do can steal us out of Jesus' hand; but we are free to let go his hand ourselves, if we're really that stupid.

EVIL THINGS IN THE WORLD

How many times does God cry about the state of the world?

'Here is tonight's news. Fighting breaks out again in Eastern Europe... A teacher is knifed to death in a school playground... Crime figures up again... A new famine in Africa...' It makes us want to weep, but how does God feel about it?

Jesus is our window into God's feelings. When his friend, Lazarus, died young, he cried. When he saw how upset everyone else was, it churned him up again (see John 11:35,38). God shares our tears and our distress at losing anything or anyone we love. He cares about everything he has made. Jesus said that even a sparrow couldn't die without God being involved (see Matthew 10:29), so he must cry out every time ANYONE is hurt unfairly – not just when big tragedies hit the headlines.

If you are hurting in any way at all, Jesus feels it with you. He loves you and cares about you and wants to share your pain with you. Tell him all about it.

Why doesn't God stop all the suffering?

He is going to. In the next life nothing will hurt or destroy; there will be no more death, sadness, crying or pain (see Isaiah 11:9; Revelation 21:4).

Why doesn't God stop suffering NOW? Because he has told US, his people, to stop it.

He has told us not to murder, have sex outside marriage, steal, tell lies or be jealous (see Exodus 20:13–17). Think how much suffering that would cut out if we obeyed him.

He told us to love and help the people round us (see Leviticus 19:18; Galatians 6:10), not quarrel with them, swear at them, spread gossip about them or leave them to face their problems alone. Think how much happier life would be if we obeyed.

He told us to look after people in need; to be understanding with those who are sad; to feed the hungry; to invite lonely people to stay; to give clothes to those who can't afford their own; to visit hospitals and prisons (see Luke 10:30–37; Romans 12:15; Matthew 25:34–45).

We can't ALL do ALL of these ALL at once! And we'll never get rid of ALL suffering in this life. But think what a wave of healing and happiness would wash over the world if every Christian obeyed just one of these instructions every day!

We ask, 'Why doesn't God stop the rot?' He says, 'Why don't YOU do it?' It's what we are here for, and his Spirit is with us to make our efforts do some good.

Who is the devil?

The devil is real.

Lots of people have given up believing in him. They think he's just a pretend figure like Father Christmas or the tooth fairy. But Jesus and the rest of the Bible say that the devil is a real person. Not a HUMAN person you can see: he is an invisible spirit (like God); but (also like God) he is really there.

The devil is invisible like God but that's where the similarity ends. He is God's arch-enemy. His name 'SATAN' means 'enemy'. He works full-time to spoil everything God has made, and to stop everything God wants to do. He has a hand in everything that is evil in the world – crime,

Bible Bit

David learnt in his own suffering that God cares:

> He does not ignore those in trouble.
> He doesn't hide from them
> but listens when they call out to him.

In the same psalm, David describes what he suffered. As we read it, we suddenly realise that Jesus suffered in the same way (see Mark 15:12–37). He is not a God who watches from the side-lines. He came and suffered with us:

> People make fun of me and hate me.
> Those who look at me laugh.
> They stick out their tongues and shake their heads.
> They say, 'Turn to the LORD for help.
> Maybe he will save you...'
> My strength has dried up like a clay pot,
> and my tongue sticks to the top of my mouth.
> You laid me in the dust of death.
> Evil people have surrounded me;
> like dogs they have trapped me.
> They have bitten my arms and legs.
> I can count all my bones;
> people look and stare at me.
> They divided my clothes among them,
> and they threw lots for my clothing.

James sums up what God expects of us:

> Religion that God accepts as pure and without fault is this: caring for orphans or widows who need help, and keeping yourself free from the world's evil influence.

suffering, pollution, illness, war. Other people have a hand in them too; but the devil is only too happy to help them along.

Because he is God's enemy, the devil is also the enemy of Christians as God's people. He makes life as hard as he can for us. He is one of the reasons why every Christian finds it a struggle to live the way Jesus wants us to.

The devil has two main ways of attacking us. The first is to tempt us to do wrong. He is always on at us: 'Go on, take it. No one will notice it's missing…' 'Copy her homework. She always does better than you…' 'Swear back at them! You don't want them to think you're weak, do you?'

Then, when we give in, he starts on weapon number two: he accuses us. The word 'DEVIL' means 'accuser'. He says, 'Huh, call yourself a Christian! You're no good. God won't forgive you for that. He'll give up on you.'

What does the devil look like?

You sometimes see little toy models of him bouncing up and down in car back windows. They make him look like a Hallowe'en character – black robe and tights, horns on his head, a long tail and carrying a pitchfork.

But this is just a figure of fun, and he certainly doesn't look like that. The Bible seems to say that the devil was once an angel in heaven who rebelled against God and who persuaded a lot of other angels to rebel too. So I guess he looks however angels look.

We don't usually see him at all in this life, any more than we see angels or God. His normal way of working is quite invisible, as he plants lying, tempting thoughts in our minds. One thing he often does, though, is use what other people say to us as a way of sneaking his temptations into us.

Jesus found this happening to him. He told his circle of friends that he would have to clash with the Jewish leaders and be put to death because he was claiming to be God's King. At once Peter said, 'God save you from those things, Lord! Those things will never happen to you!'

Jesus realised that the devil was using Peter's words to

try to stop him carrying out God's plan. He said to Peter, 'GO AWAY FROM ME, SATAN! You are not helping me! You don't care about the things of God, but only about the things people think are important' (Matthew 16:22–23).

Though Jesus looked at Peter, he spoke to Satan. So I guess the devil sometimes 'looks like' the people round us, even our friends. When they tell lies, he tempts us to do the same; when they say something hurtful or cruel about other

Bible Bit

We learn a lot about the devil in the last book of the Bible. It is like a series of dreams, with the devil appearing as a dragon and Jesus as a lamb:

> Then there was a war in heaven. Michael and his angels fought against the dragon, and the dragon and his angels fought back. But the dragon was not strong enough, and he and his angels lost their place in heaven. The giant dragon was thrown down out of heaven. (He is that old snake called the devil or Satan, who tricks the whole world.) The dragon with his angels was thrown down to the earth.
>
> Then I heard a loud voice in heaven saying:
> 'The salvation and the power and the kingdom of our God
>   and the authority of his Christ have now come.
> The accuser of our brothers and sisters,
>   who accused them day and night before our God,
>   has been thrown down.
> And our brothers and sisters defeated him
>   by the blood of the Lamb's death
>   and by the message they preached...
> But it will be terrible for the earth and the sea,
>   because the devil has come down to you!
> He is filled with anger,
>   because he knows he does not have much time.'

people at school, the devil pushes us to join in. He uses their words to try to get us to do wrong things or take a wrong turning. Be on the look-out.

How do you know when things are wrong? How can you tell when it's the devil tempting you?

Nine times out of ten, we KNOW when something is wrong. Our conscience tells us we're going against what is good and what God wants. God has given us the Bible to show us what he wants. Learning to love and care as he does is right. Cheating and hating and cruelty are always wrong.

Occasionally, though, we're not sure. We want to do

something but we don't know whether it's right or wrong. Does this feeling of doubt come from God or the devil? There is a helpful way to find out. God has put an example of the devil's tactics on record for us (see Genesis 2:16–17; 3:1–5).

The devil often goes about tempting us the same way he did with the first human beings in the Garden of Eden. God put them in this perfect environment and gave them just one commandment and warning: 'You may eat the fruit from any tree in the garden, BUT YOU MUST NOT EAT THE FRUIT FROM THE TREE which gives the knowledge of good and evil. IF YOU EVER EAT FRUIT FROM THAT TREE, YOU WILL DIE!'

The devil set about attacking God's law in four ways. If you ever hear a voice saying these same things, you can be pretty sure it is the devil having a go at you.

1 He cast doubt on it.

'Did God REALLY SAY that you must not eat fruit...?' God wants us to trust him, but the devil is behind every idea that makes us doubt and worry.

2 He exaggerated it.

'Did God really say that you must not eat fruit from ANY TREE IN THE GARDEN?' God only banned one tree, but

Bible Bit

Paul gives us the good news that the devil's temptations are under God's control:

> Every test that you have experienced is the kind that normally comes to people. But God keeps his promise, and he will not allow you to be tested beyond your power to remain firm; at the time you are put to the test, he will give you the strength to endure it, and so provide you with a way out.

the devil loves to put it around that God is a mean old grump. This is an idea we still keep hearing today. In fact, God only wants what's best for us: he offers to keep us safe from anything that would harm us.

3 He denied it.

'YOU WILL NOT DIE.' Now the devil does the exact opposite of the last one. He says God is too soft to carry out his threat. You would be a fool to believe him. God is totally true. He keeps his promises AND HIS WARNINGS. Any idea that goes against this comes from the devil.

4 He explained it away.

'God knows that if you eat the fruit from that tree, you will learn about good and evil AND YOU WILL BE LIKE GOD!' In other words, God is unfair. He's keeping the goodies to himself and hiding them from you. When he wants us to go against God, the devil will always find some good-sounding reason why we shouldn't believe or obey what God has said to us: 'Nobody believes that nowadays. It went out with the dinosaurs', etc, etc.

This is what the devil's ideas sound like. But if what you are thinking of helps you believe in God better, love him more and come closer to him, it sounds good to me.

Is the devil more powerful than God?

Definitely not. God has already thrown him out of heaven, and when he sets up the new earth he is going to finish the devil off for good (see Revelation 20:10).

Why does God allow him to carry on?

It seems God has two reasons for letting the devil keep up his bad work on earth. One is to give people the choice of joining forces with God, or with his enemies.

The other is to allow Christians to grow stronger by

being part of the battle between good and evil. Every time we turn the devil's temptations down, we strike a blow for God. At the same time, we gain strength through our resistance, and next time we are more likely to win again. Try resisting the temptation to swear or gossip or whatever your usual pitfall is.

Meanwhile, God keeps strict limits on what the devil can do. He won't allow him to tempt us beyond our breaking point. And the devil's time on earth is limited.

Bible Bit
The shortest instruction in the Bible on how to treat the devil comes from James:

Stand against the devil, and the devil will run from you.

What do ouija boards do?

Ouija boards look like a board game, marked out with the letters of the alphabet and YES and NO spaces. The idea is to ask the spirit of someone who has died to answer questions about the next life or the future in this life. You rest your fingers on a pointer or upside-down glass on the board, and they turn it towards YES or NO; or they spell out the answer, letter by letter.

This is one of many ways of telling people's fortunes, like star signs, palm-reading and tarot cards. They are often called 'OCCULT', which means 'hidden' or using invisible, supernatural powers. The question is, are those powers good or evil?

Sometimes, I guess, the alien powers aren't really there. There are times when the board doesn't work at all, and that is probably because everyone is treating it as a joke. Even when it does appear to work, there aren't necessarily any supernatural spirits answering. There is something fishy even about the name 'OUIJA'. It just means 'Yes-yes' ('Yes' in French, 'Yes' in German). When it does give an

Bible Bit

God's law makes it very clear what he wants:

> Don't let anyone use magic or witchcraft, or try to explain the meaning of signs. Don't let anyone try to control others with magic, and don't let them be mediums or try to talk with the spirits of dead people. The LORD hates anyone who does these things.

'Mediums' are people who say they can contact the dead, and often act like a human radio receiver for the dead person's voice. The prophet Isaiah explains why God's people don't need to contact the dead:

> Some people say, 'Ask the mediums and fortune-tellers, who whisper and mutter, what to do.' But I tell you that people should ask their God for help. Why should people who are still alive ask something from the dead? You should follow the teachings and the agreement with the LORD. The mediums and fortune-tellers do not speak the word of the LORD, so their words are worth nothing.

answer, it is usually the nice, comforting news you want to hear. 'Is that the spirit of my cousin who died?' YES. 'Are you in heaven?' YES. 'Are you happy there?' YES.

One thing is certain – this is not your Cousin Kerry. Dead people don't come back to talk to the living (see Ecclesiastes 9:6; Hebrews 9:27). It MAY not be anyone or anything at all. Our subconscious wishes are very strong. They are quite able to make us turn the pointer to the answer we want without us realising what's going on.

This doesn't mean that it's all just a harmless game or joke. God says very strongly that his people must have nothing to do with it. I think this is because sometimes (perhaps most times) the devil and his evil spirits join in the 'game'. The harm they can do us is no joke at all.

Jesus called the devil 'a liar and the father of lies'. He is always telling lies to mislead us. If he says he is Cousin Kerry having a lovely time in heaven, he is luring us on to forget what God says and disobey it.

The apostle Paul said, 'Don't give the Devil a chance' (see Ephesians 4:27). That means ouija sessions are out for Christians. If we deliberately disobey, we lay ourselves open to the devil interfering with our lives, maybe even controlling them. Some people find themselves unable to stop lying or abusing other people or attacking Christians.

This isn't something to be afraid of, if you are a true Christian. If you love Jesus and follow him – which, of course, means doing what he says – he will keep you safe from all harm. His close friend, John, said, 'God's Spirit, who is in you, is greater than the devil' (see 1 John 4:4).

Further ??? to think about by yourself or discuss with friends

1 What one new thing could you DO to help cut down suffering in the world? It doesn't matter how short or small your action is; every little bit counts. But make sure you do SOMETHING!

2 What one new thing could you do to help drive the devil back? No matter how small, make sure you do it.

3 If you have any other questions or ideas, write them in the space below.

WHAT HAPPENS AFTER WE DIE?

Does absolutely every non-Christian go to hell? What about nice people who aren't Christians?

True or false?

If you're good and kind, you'll go to heaven. But if you do more wrong than right, you'll go to hell.

False! Wrong! Rubbish! The Bible doesn't say this at all.

The Bible says God is perfect, and nothing imperfect can go near him. He is red-hot purity and burns up anything impure. If you think of your life like an exam, he doesn't accept C grades, or B grades, or even most A* grades. His pass-mark is 100 per cent; anything less and we can't get in.

We like to think that big crimes (like murder or rape) are worse than the things we all do (like being selfish or jealous). We hope God won't mind our few small bad points.

This is not how God sees things. Of course, he thinks murder and rape are terrible, but so are selfishness and jealousy. Jesus said the two greatest of God's laws are:

1 Love God above everything else.
2 Love everyone else as you love yourself.

If we have ever broken these laws, we have committed the greatest sins in God's book.

It's no good saying, 'I'm really nice to my friends most of the time.' Or 'I'll give all my money to buy guide dogs for blind people.' There is nothing we can do to make up for the past. We're not perfect; we have scored less than 100 per cent; so we have ruled ourselves out of going to heaven.

This means we're all bound to go to hell. Hell is where you go if you don't go to heaven. It means never getting into God's home.

'But hang on, slow down a minute. Don't Christians believe they'll go to heaven when they die.'

Yes, they do and they will. But not because they have been good. ONLY BECAUSE GOD HAS FORGIVEN THEM.

God loves us. He wants us to be part of his family, to know him now and live in his home when we die. He couldn't bear the idea that we had blown it and shut ourselves out of heaven. So he became one of us and lived on earth as Jesus. He lived the one 100 per cent perfect life there has ever been. When he died on the cross, he took the penalty we deserve for doing wrong. So now he can offer to forgive us – wash us clean – and give us a new start in life.

He did this for everyone who has ever lived. Absolutely no one needs to go to hell.

Christians are people who have said 'Yes' to God's offer to forgive us. 'Sorry for going wrong. Thank you for dying for me. Please take me on as a child in your family who will belong to you for ever.' Jesus said that, as his followers, we are as good as in heaven already: 'I give them eternal life, and they will never die' (see John 10:28).

Where does that leave people who aren't Christians? If they have heard about Jesus but turned away from him, then obviously they haven't said 'Yes' to him. Even if they have heard about Jesus but done nothing about him, they haven't said 'Yes'. So they haven't received God's forgiveness. They haven't taken the one and only exit marked

'Heaven'. They are still on the motorway heading for hell. They desperately need rescuing. Who is going to care about them and keep reminding them about Jesus except us? We need to pray for them, and see if there are ways we can keep them in touch with the Christian good news.

When my best friend left school, he wasn't a Christian, even though I had been praying for him and pestering him about it for two years! He was going to study French at college, so he went off to spend the summer in France and said he wouldn't read a word of English till he got back. He was dropping a heavy hint that it would be no good lending him any more of my Christian books. But I wasn't scuppered that easily. I found my old French dictionary and borrowed a French Bible and wrote him letters about Christianity in dreadful French. A few months later he became a Christian (probably out of exhaustion!) and since then he has helped lots of others to become Christians too.

It is different for people who have never heard about Jesus. Obviously, they can't start following him if they don't know who he is. And they can't thank him for dying for them, if they don't know that he did!

We don't know what will happen to them, BUT GOD DOES. Thank goodness it is HIS job to work out who goes to heaven, not ours. I guess he will judge people who have never heard about Jesus on their attitude. If they think they're quite OK as they are, he will leave them as they are. They deserve to go to hell like the rest of us because they have broken God's law. But if they're crying out to whatever God there is to forgive them, surely he will. Jesus died for them even though they don't know it yet.

What if you sincerely believe in another god? Will you still go to heaven?

Well, yes and no.

No, if you think it is enough to be a Hindu or Muslim or whatever. No one goes to heaven because they are religious

Bible Bit

These may be Jesus' own words, or those of his friend, John, putting what Jesus taught another way:

> 'God loved the world so much that he gave his one and only Son so that whoever believes in him may not be lost, but have eternal life.'

This is definitely Jesus speaking:

> 'I am the way, and the truth, and the life. The only way to the Father is through me.'

or sincere, any more than because they're nice. It's a good thing to be sincere, but you can be sincerely wrong. Lots of people supported Hitler when he came to power. They sincerely believed he would do Germany nothing but good. It steadily became all too clear they had backed the wrong horse.

According to Jesus (who certainly knows), other religions are wrong horses for getting into heaven. He said the only way in is through him, because he died to put right the wrong things we have done. There is no one in any other religion who did anything like it – not Moses, not Muhammad, not the Buddha.

So there are only two ways that people from other religions will end up in heaven. EITHER they have heard about Jesus and put their trust in him. OR they haven't heard about him, but know they need someone to take away the wall they have built between them and God by the wrong things they have done, said and thought.

I once got talking with someone in the launderette. When he said he was a Muslim, I thought (may God forgive me), 'This is the opposition. He'll be very anti-Christian.' But I plucked up my courage and told him I was a Christian. 'Oh, I love Jesus,' he said. I gawped at him as he went on, 'Our religion tells us about Jesus. He's not like Muhammad. He forgave the people he met. I love him very much. When I do something bad, I pray to Jesus for forgiveness.'

He hadn't yet understood everything about Jesus. At that time he was still a Muslim. But I think he was already on his way to heaven. He had sensed that Jesus was the way in.

Do you go to heaven or hell if you die when you are a baby?

The Bible doesn't tell us for sure. Once again, we have got to leave it to God. He knows what sort of person the baby had it in her or him to be. He knows whether the baby would have loved Jesus or not if he or she had grown old enough to learn about him.

One thing I do know for sure – Jesus loves babies. He went out of his way to cuddle small children and bless them. He said God's kingdom belongs to people like them (see Mark 10:13–16). Children haven't yet grown full of themselves, trying to run their own lives. They have to be what we should all really be – totally dependent on God.

If you commit suicide, will you go to hell even if you were a nice person?

You would only ever kill yourself if you felt trapped with no hope of escape. Sadly, many people do commit suicide each year; some believe in God, others don't. But no Christian ever needs to feel that hopeless. We have handed control of our lives over to Jesus, so we leave it to him to decide when we die. In the meantime, he promises to look after us and make our lives really worthwhile (see John 10:9–11,27–28).

I can't imagine any Christian committing suicide unless they were emotionally disturbed or mentally ill. God would understand if they were, and he wouldn't hold it against them. They would still go to heaven because they had received his forgiveness. This may be why the Bible never lists taking your own life as a sin deserving punishment.

Bible Bit

Paul told the Christians at Rome to use their lives to serve Jesus; this would seem to rule out suicide:

> So brothers and sisters, since God has shown us great mercy, I beg you to offer your lives as a living sacrifice to him.

At that time people were used to the idea of sacrificing dead animals to their gods. This was a new idea, to serve God by staying alive.

What is hell like?

Hell is the opposite of heaven. Heaven is where God and Jesus are; hell is where they aren't. There is nothing good about hell at all. This is why Jesus sometimes called it 'the darkness'.

He also called it the place 'where the fire never goes out'. I hope and think he doesn't mean an actual inferno, but rather a state of mind which is like fire. People in hell will realise they have totally wasted their chance to get to know God and serve him. They will know they have thrown themselves away into the incinerator. What a tragedy!

Some people think the 'fire' will burn up the people in hell and obliterate them. If this is true, they are destroyed – lost and gone for ever – but at least they know nothing more about it.

I hope they may be right. But Jesus says the fire never goes out, and that sounds horribly as if people go on knowing for ever what they have done to themselves by telling God to keep out of their lives.

Either way, I find hell a terrifying thought. I can never

stop thanking Jesus for rescuing me from hell, and I want to spend my life helping other people escape from it too. The way to escape is to belong to Jesus and to follow him.

One of my Christian heroes was called Charles Studd. He played cricket for England and later became a missionary in China and Africa. He couldn't bear to spend all his time with other Christians when there were people who hadn't even heard about Jesus. He wrote a short poem to express his life's ambition:

> **Some like to live within the sound**
> **Of church or chapel bell.**
> **I want to run a rescue shop**
> **Within a yard of hell.**

Bible Bit

Jesus warns us to make sure that we don't go to hell:

> **'Enter through the narrow gate. The gate is wide and the road is wide that leads to hell, and many people enter through that gate. But the gate is small and the road is narrow that leads to true life. Only a few people find that road.'**

What is heaven like? What do we do all day? I don't want to be just a zombie.

You can stop straining in front of a mirror to see if your back is sprouting wings. And pack up the harp lessons. The Bible says nothing about floating around on clouds in heaven. It is time to get a bit clearer what it DOES say.

First of all, heaven is where God lives now. It isn't a place in the universe, but a whole other dimension of reality which our human eyes can't see. But this isn't where we shall spend the next life. The Bible says Jesus is going to bring everything that's wrong on earth to an end – and then remake it. We're going to spend eternity not in heaven but on an earth made perfect! Not some airy-fairy spirit world above the bright blue sky, but a solid, down-to-earth place where we shall feel at home.

Life then will be like it is now – only better. It will be life WITHOUT THE BAD BITS. Just think of it! There will be no more accidents, bombs, cruelty, dying... (Now you fill in the rest of the alphabet.)

No more...

e	f
g	h
i	j
k	l
m	n
o	p
q	r
s	t
u	v
w	x
y	z

I hope this makes you feel better already.

But the new world won't just be a censored version of the old. It will also be life WITH EXTRA GOOD BITS.

It isn't singing choruses and twiddling our thumbs for ever. We certainly won't be zombies. Life on the new earth will be better in every way than now. We'll be more alive than ever before.

There will be work to do, tough work, but really enjoyable – Jesus compared it to being in charge of several cities (Luke 19:12–13,15–19). Just think of the challenge that would be! Helping to look after communities of thousands, perhaps millions, of people. Keeping them and the places where they live and work and play in good condition, up to God's standards. Making them beautiful, worthy of the owner. And they will be cities without the bad bits of cities now: no overcrowding, no pollution, no vandalism. Plenty of fresh air and open countryside included.

There would be any number of jobs to choose from: agriculture, building, cooking, design… (Again, fill in the rest of the alphabet.)

Other jobs might be...

e	f
g	h
i	j
k	l
m	n
o	p
q	r
s	t
u	v
w	x
y	z

Don't forget different kinds of fun and games and entertainment. There would even be a place for people who DO want to play the harp!

We will love it. It will give us total job-satisfaction. It's the work we were designed to do. Taking care of the new world, helping it work properly, making it pleased to know us. This time we'll make a really good job of it. Not like the mess we've made of the old earth.

Best of all, the next life will be life WITH JESUS.

A younger Christian friend once visited an old man who knew he was dying. She offered to read him something from the Bible. 'Yes please,' he said. 'John chapter 14.'

She started reading Jesus' words: 'Don't let your hearts be troubled… There are many rooms in my Father's house.'

She stopped and smiled. 'Isn't that wonderful?' she said.

'No, go on,' he said. 'That's not the best bit.'

So she read on. 'I am going there to prepare a place for you.'

She stopped again. 'That must be it,' she thought. 'What

a wonderful comfort for the old boy.'

'Go on, go on,' he said. 'You're still not there.'

She turned quickly back to what Jesus was saying. 'After I go and prepare a place for you, I will come back and take you to be with me so that you may be where I am.'

The old man lay back and smiled. 'THAT'S it,' he sighed. 'I want to be with him.'

Jesus will be there with us. We'll see him and know him, love him and serve him. In him we'll find everything we ever wanted.

I guess we will never run out of things to do or of the fun in doing them. School work and Sunday services may get boring in this life, but it won't be like that in the world to come. Not when you see Jesus face to face, and the angels lead the song and dance group, and the world is full of people who love Jesus, and some of them are people you have always wanted to meet, or meet again, and there is time and space to do everything at the right time and pace – and you will be doing what you want to do anyway, and you are back in touch with the God who made you and loves you, and you will be with him for ever and ever and ever...

'What does Jesus mean by "many rooms"?'

When Jesus came to the old earth, there wasn't a room for him in the hotel. He had to be born in the cowshed. If you belong to him, then when you come to the new earth, you won't be stuck outside in the cold. There will be a room with your name on it, perhaps a whole house or flat; or perhaps we'll be sharing with friends and family. However many millions of friends Jesus has, there will be room for them all. We'll have the whole earth to fill!

Bible Bit

The Bible ends with John's vision of the future – heaven on earth:

> Then I saw a new heaven and a new earth ... I heard a loud voice from the throne, saying, 'Now God's presence is with people, and he will live with them, and they will be his people. God himself will be with them and will be their God. He will wipe away every tear from their eyes, and there will be no more death, sadness, crying or pain, because all the old ways are gone.'
>
> Nothing that God judges guilty will be in that city. The throne of God and of the Lamb will be there, and God's servants will worship him ... There will never be night again. They will not need the light of a lamp or the light of the sun, because the Lord God will give them light. And they will rule as kings forever and ever.

'How can God supply the light?'

How does God supply light on the old earth? He uses the sun and electricity or candles. But he doesn't need to use artificial lights like these – he is much brighter and more glorious himself. It's just that for now he keeps himself under wraps because his rays would dazzle and blind us.

On the new earth, God will be there in person with his power switched full on. And he will give us stronger eyes to be able to look at him and love him.

'If there is no night, when are we going to sleep?'

I don't think there will be any sleep. We'll be much too busy and happy to want to miss a second of it. I stayed up working the whole night before one of my exams, but then fell asleep during it! The teacher in charge saw me slumped over the table, but left me for about twenty minutes because he thought I was praying for inspiration! In the end he realised what had happened and woke me up, but it was too late to make up the lost time.

Our bodies need sleep on this earth to restore energy. But, on the new earth, work won't be tiring and our bodies won't grow old or wear out. We'll all have super-powers; and we'll be in constant contact with the Power Supply!

Will we get what we want in heaven?

Yes – and no. It won't be like a mega Christmas tree, with all the prezzies we wanted but never got the first time round. I guess we won't mind about that because we won't still want the same things. There may not be many magazines or CDs or personal computers on the new earth. Or there may be – I don't know. But they won't seem as important as they do here and now.

Why not? Because what we will want most of all is exactly what we will get. The chance to be with God and all his other friends, loving and serving them – for ever.

Do we still have relationships with our friends and families in heaven? Will I see my parents again?

If they are Christians – or if they end their lives trusting God – they will be there with us in the new world.

I don't know whether we will live with our families as before, or in the same neighbourhood as our old friends.

But I feel sure that we will SEE them. We will be there for ever, after all. There is bound to be time to go and visit them, even if they're living in a different area. And, if Jesus knew what he was talking about, there are going to be parties in God's kingdom where we will meet all sorts of interesting people!

Bible Bit

Jesus told Jews they wouldn't have the new world to themselves:

'Many people will come from the east and the west and will sit and eat with Abraham, Isaac, and Jacob in the kingdom of heaven.'

What happens when we die?

If we die before the end of the world, our brains and bodies pack up. That's the part of us that gets buried or cremated (burnt in a special incinerator).

But our invisible spirits live on. Exactly what happens next I'm not quite sure – yet! There are two ideas which Christians have, and both seem to have a basis in the Bible.

One is that we go into a sort of 'cold storage' which the Bible calls sleep. We stay unconscious until Jesus comes back to end the old world and start the new. This is the next thing we are aware of after dying.

The other idea is that the moment we die, we go to be

with Jesus in heaven. Or, perhaps more accurately, in a special part of heaven which Jesus called paradise (see Luke 23:43). If so, this is only a half-time break before the real fun begins and Jesus returns to earth.

Either way, it is at this point that we will get new bodies to live in. So it won't matter if our old bodies were burnt or damaged through illness or violent death. Our new bodies will be better altogether, and perfectly designed for the new earth (see 1 Corinthians 15:35–57).

Bible Bit

In the following verses Paul, Silas and Timothy seem to be saying that we all have to wait for Jesus to come back:

> **The Lord himself will come down from heaven ... And those who have died believing in Christ will rise first. After that, we who are still alive will be gathered up with them in the clouds to meet the Lord in the air.**

But later Paul wrote that he would be joining Jesus in heaven:

> **I want to leave this life and be with Christ, which is much better, but you need me here in my body.**

I'm sure Paul knew exactly what he meant, but I haven't worked it out yet!

Are you sad if you leave someone you love behind?

The last exam had just finished. I walked out into the street in a daze. My last term at college was over. Suddenly, I heard heavy footsteps running after me. 'Lance, Lance!' a voice bellowed.

I turned round. It was the man I'd shared a flat with for

the last two years. 'I've just thought,' he said. 'I'm never going to see you again – till heaven!'

To begin with, I laughed. Then it hit me that he might be right. Supposing I never saw him again till after we were both dead? A great wave of sadness swept over me and I started to cry. I couldn't stop myself.

It is even worse when someone dies and you really lose them. The person left on earth is sad, but I imagine the one who dies also feels some of the pain of the relationship being cut off.

If you are both Christians, you know that you're going to see each other again. In the meantime, if you had died, I think you would be kept pretty busy with all the new people you meet. Including Jesus.

Do we have memories of earth in heaven?

Jesus came back to life after he had died. He didn't go to heaven straightaway, but showed himself to his friends on earth. He knew who they were and remembered what he had taught them (see John 20:16; 21:15–17; Luke 24:44). He said he would listen out for their prayers (see John 14:14). I think he was giving us a glimpse of what life will be like in the next world. So yes, I think we will have memories of life on earth.

When Jesus comes back to earth, he will judge people on all they've said and done (see Matthew 12:36–37; John 5:27–29). A lot of wrongs will be put right. It is really annoying when we get accused of things we didn't do, or people don't believe our version of what happened. Jesus knows the truth, and he will set the record straight. He can prove we were right – or perhaps sometimes wrong! His perfect memory may need to correct ours on some details.

But when we start on the new earth, there are some things we won't remember any more. From the way God put it to Isaiah, I think we will forget all the sad, unpleasant things in life – things like illness or divorce or rape –

because they won't be there any more. At last we will be able to put them out of our minds.

Bible Bit

God tells Isaiah about the new world:

'Look, I will make new heavens and a new earth,
   and people will not remember the past
   or think about those things.
My people will be happy forever
   because of the things I will make...
There will never again be heard in that city
   the sounds of crying and sadness.
There will never be a baby from that city
   who lives only a few days.
And there will never be an older person
   who doesn't have a long life.'

Can we see what's happening on earth?

God can. He sees everything (see Hebrews 4:13).

So, if we go to be with him in paradise when we die, perhaps we too will be able to see how things are going back on earth. How are they getting on without us? Do they miss us? What are they saying about us?!

Or perhaps not. God may have other things for us to look at. The sight of what goes on in heaven sounds pretty mind-blowing to me.

Will we be able to have relationships that are more than just friendships? Do you get boy-girl relationships in heaven when you want them?

According to Jesus, we won't get married (see Mark 12:25). We won't need to. For one thing, we will all live for ever, so there won't be any new babies born. In any case, we won't be limited to a close relationship with just one person at a time. We won't be shy or jealous or prejudiced any more.

On earth Sharon felt she was a poor copy of her mum and her elder sister. She thought other people were always laughing at her or criticising her. She clung to her boyfriend because he was the only one who encouraged her and made her feel good. But in the new world she will find that she is able to have happy, trusting relationships with everyone she knows.

Tim was quite different. He had grown up with a very sunny nature. He was fun to be with and everyone loved him. He used to joke he could never get married because he had too many girlfriends to choose between. In the end, though, he fell in love with Jasmine and they lived happily ever… Well yes, they were happy. But he always felt a slight twinge at how many friends he had lost touch with once he settled down and the kids came along.

In the new world, I think there will be time and space for everyone we love. We will enjoy and care deeply for ALL the boys/girls, men/women we are with. Every friendship will be special, but it won't be private, cutting other people out. We will want to share ourselves with everyone else.

Bible Bit

Some of John's visions in the last book of the Bible show us what it is like in heaven now before the new world begins:

> Before me was a throne in heaven, and someone was sitting on it. The One who sat on the throne looked like precious stones, like jasper and carnelian. All around the throne was a rainbow the colour of an emerald ... Lightning flashes and noises and thundering came from the throne.

Do animals go to heaven or hell?

The short answer is, we don't know. The Bible doesn't say for sure.

But it is very hard to imagine animals going to hell, in the sense of a place of punishment for breaking God's laws. We assume that it is instinct which makes lions kill for food or rabbits mate with any available partner. As far as we know, they don't say to themselves, 'I know God doesn't like murder or sleeping around, but who cares?' You can't blame them for something they've never learnt to see as wrong.

But what about animals in 'heaven' (the new earth)? Some people say they don't want to go to heaven if their

Bible Bit

Figures like animals appear in John's vision or dream of what heaven is like before the world is made new:

> In the centre and around (God's) throne were four living creatures with eyes all over them, in front and in back. The first living creature was like a lion. The second was like a calf. The third had a face like a man. The fourth was like a flying eagle. Each of these four living creatures had six wings and was covered all over with eyes, inside and out. Day and night they never stop saying:
> 'Holy, holy, holy, is the Lord God Almighty.
> He was, he is, and he is coming.'

Animals also feature in Isaiah's picture of life on the new earth when God's new King (Jesus) takes charge:

> Then wolves will live in peace with lambs,
> and leopards will lie down to rest with goats.
> Calves, lions and young bulls will eat together,
> and a little child will lead them.
> Cows and bears will eat together in peace.
> Their young will lie down to rest together.
> Lions will eat hay as oxen do.

puppy or budgie or goldfish isn't there. I think they need to understand two things:

1 It's not up to us to choose who will be in the new world.

God has found a way to make it possible for us to be there, at the terrible cost of Jesus going through the God-forsakenness of hell instead of us (see Mark 15:34). We are unbelievably lucky to be forgiven and make it into the perfect new heaven on earth. I'm sure our main feeling will be amazed thanks that WE are there, and not complaining about anyone or anything that isn't.

2 The new earth will be better than the old one.

Our pets may be there: it is possible that God will bring them back to life in the love we feel for them. But it is also possible that he won't, if he made them only to be part of the old world. The one thing we can be sure of is that if – and I only say IF – our animal-friends aren't there, it will only be because our lives will be filled with even better and more loving friends.

Will those friends just be Jesus and other people and angels? Or will they include animals? My guess is they will. The Bible pictures the new earth with animals on it, though I don't know for sure whether they are real animals, or just pictures to give us a feel of something we can't yet understand.

If there are animals on the old earth, it seems to me more than likely they will be there in the new one. God is planning to put the world back into its original perfect running order. According to his version of how he made it in the first place, he put the animals there before even the human beings. And he liked them (see Genesis 1:20–25).

Further ??? to think about by yourself or discuss with friends

1 If you had to die tonight, what are some of the things you would miss most?

2 What are some of the things you look forward to and hope for in the new world?

3 If God was sitting and talking with you now, what are some of the questions you would like to ask him about the future? Write them in the space below.

Is there anyone else you could discuss them with?

4 What are some of the questions you want to ask God when you do meet him? Write them in the space below.

HELPLINE

'How do you know if you have – or haven't – got a relationship with God?'

If you're not sure, here's a prayer you could pray:

> **Dear God, I'm not sure whether I really know you, but I want to. I know I don't deserve to know you and I'm sorry for the wrong things I've done.**
>
> **Thank you that Jesus died on the cross so you could forgive me and let me come to know you.**
>
> **Please now come in on my life by your Holy Spirit and make me your friend and child. Amen.**

If you have said that prayer and meant it, God has heard and answered. You may not feel any different straightaway, but he will make himself known to you over the next days and weeks.

Is there someone among your friends or family whom you could tell about praying this prayer? Someone who will help you get to know God better?

'I'm too busy to stop and pray...' & 'How can God speak to me through the Bible?'

Scripture Union's *One Up* notes to help you read the Bible are available from many churches, all Christian bookshops, and by post from:

* Scripture Union, PO Box 764, Oxford, OX4 5FJ; tel 01865 747669, fax 01865 747568.

'What if your church is really boring?'

Some people who can help you start or support a church youth group or school Christian Union are:

- Pathfinders, CPAS, Athena Drive, Tachbrook Park, Warwick CV34 6NG; tel 01926 337613.
- Youth for Christ, Cleobury Place, Cleobury Mortimer, Kidderminster DY14 8JG; tel 01299 271158.
- Scripture Union in Schools, 207-209 Queensway, Bletchley MK2 2EB; tel 01908 856000.

'If you have been abused for years and you kill the person who was abusing you, is that right or wrong?'

If you have suffered abuse and don't know who else to turn to, contact:

- Childline, Freepost 1111, London EC4B 4BB; Freephone 0800 1111.
- NSPCC (National Society for the Prevention of Cruelty to Children), 42 Curtain Road, London EC2A 3NH; Freephone 0800 800500.

'Shouldn't people with AIDS have the same rights?'

The main Christian charities helping people with AIDS are:

- ACET (AIDS Care Education and Training), PO Box 3693, London SW15 2BQ; tel 0181-780 0400.
- Mildmay Mission Hospital, Hackney Road, Shoreditch, London E2 7NA; tel 0171-739 2331.

If you have any questions about AIDS or HIV, please ring the National AIDS Helpline tel 0800 567123. It is free and private.